WEB 2017

The Fifth International Conference on Building and Exploring Web Based Environments

May 21 - 25, 2017

Barcelona, Spain

WEB 2017 Editors

Carla Merkle Westphall, University of Santa Catarina, Brazil

Daniela Marghitu, Auburn University, USA

Printed from e-media with permission by:

Curran Associates, Inc.
57 Morehouse Lane
Red Hook, NY 12571

Some format issues inherent in the e-media version may also appear in this print version.

Printed by Curran Associates, Inc. (2017)

International Academy, Research, and Industry Association (IARIA)
412 Derby Way
Wilmington, DE 19810

Phone: (408) 893-6407
Fax: (408) 527-6351

petre@iaria.org

Additional copies of this publication are available from:

Curran Associates, Inc.
57 Morehouse Lane
Red Hook, NY 12571 USA
Phone: 845-758-0400
Fax: 845-758-2633
Email: curran@proceedings.com
Web: www.proceedings.com

TABLE OF CONTENTS

WEB 1: TRENDS ON WEB-BASED DATA PROCESSING/ANALYTICS

WEB 2: WEB FUNDAMENTALS

WEB 3: SEMANTIC WEB DESIGNING AND PROGRAMMING

WEB 2017

Foreword

The Fifth International Conference on Building and Exploring Web Based Environments (WEB 2017), held between May 21 - 25, 2017 - Barcelona, Spain, continued the inaugural conference on web-related theoretical and practical aspects, focusing on identifying challenges for building web-based useful services and applications, and for effectively extracting and integrating knowledge from the Web, enterprise data, and social media.

The Web has changed the way we share knowledge, the way we design distributed services and applications, the way we access large volumes of data, and the way we position ourselves with our peers.

Successful exploitation of web-based concepts by web communities lies on the integration of traditional data management techniques and semantic information into web-based frameworks and systems.

We take here the opportunity to warmly thank all the members of the WEB 2017 Technical Program Committee, as well as the numerous reviewers. The creation of such a high quality conference program would not have been possible without their involvement. We also kindly thank all the authors who dedicated much of their time and efforts to contribute to WEB 2017. We truly believe that, thanks to all these efforts, the final conference program consisted of top quality contributions.

Also, this event could not have been a reality without the support of many individuals, organizations, and sponsors. We are grateful to the members of the WEB 2017 organizing committee for their help in handling the logistics and for their work to make this professional meeting a success.

We hope that WEB 2017 was a successful international forum for the exchange of ideas and results between academia and industry and for the promotion of progress in the field of Web-based environments.

We are convinced that the participants found the event useful and communications very open. We also hope that Barcelona provided a pleasant environment during the conference and everyone saved some time for exploring this beautiful city.

WEB 2017 Chairs:

Daniela Marghitu, Auburn University, USA
Erich Schweighofer, University of Vienna - Centre for Computers and Law, Austria
Toyohide Watanabe, Nagoya Industrial Science Research Institute, Japan
Demetrios Sampson, Curtin University, Australia
Mariusz Trzaska, Polish-Japanese Academy of Information Technology, Poland
Imon Banerjee, Stanford University School of Medicine, USA
Alexiei Dingli, University of Malta, Malta
Hossein Sarrafzadeh, Unitec Institute of Technology, New Zealand
Michel Jourlin, Jean Monnet University, Saint-Etienne, France

WEB Industry/Research Advisory Committee
Taketoshi Ushiama, Kyushu University, Japan
Krzysztof Walczak, Poznan University of Economics, Poland

WEB 2017

Committee

WEB Steering Committee

Daniela Marghitu, Auburn University, USA
Erich Schweighofer, University of Vienna - Centre for Computers and Law, Austria
Toyohide Watanabe, Nagoya Industrial Science Research Institute, Japan
Demetrios Sampson, Curtin University, Australia
Mariusz Trzaska, Polish-Japanese Academy of Information Technology, Poland
Imon Banerjee, Stanford University School of Medicine, USA
Alexiei Dingli, University of Malta, Malta
Hossein Sarrafzadeh, Unitec Institute of Technology, New Zealand
Michel Jourlin, Jean Monnet University, Saint-Etienne, France

WEB Industry/Research Advisory Committee

Taketoshi Ushiama, Kyushu University, Japan
Krzysztof Walczak, Poznan University of Economics, Poland

WEB 2017 Technical Program Committee

Rocio Abascal Mena, Universidad Autónoma Metropolitana - Cuajimalpa, Mexico
Leandro Antonelli, UNLP, Argentina
Irina Astrova, Tallinn University of Technology, Estonia
Sofia Athenikos, Flipboard, USA
Dirk Bade, University of Hamburg, Germany
Stefan Bischof, Siemens AG Österreich, Austria
Carlos Bobed Lisbona, University of Zaragoza, Spain
Tharrenos Bratitsis, University of Western Macedonia, Greece
Marcin Butlewski, Poznan University of Technology, Poland
Rodrigo Capobianco Guido, Paulo State University (Unesp), Brazil
Naděžda Chalupová, Mendel University in Brno, Czech Republic
Dickson Chiu, The University of Hong Kong, Hong Kong
Bouras Christos, University of Patras, Greece
Alexiei Dingli, University of Malta, Malta
Vadim Ermolayev, Zaporozhye National University, Ukraine
Cécile Favre, University of Lyon | ERIC Lab - Lyon 2, France
Giacomo Fiumara, Università degli Studi di Messina, Italy
Jakub Flotyński, Poznań University of Economics and Business, Poland
Raffaella Folgieri, Università degli Studi di Milano, Italy
Marco Furini, University of Modena and Reggio Emilia, Italy
Christos K. Georgiadis, University of Macedonia, Greece
Abigail Goldsteen, IBM Research – Haifa, Israel
Dorian Gorgan, Technical University of Cluj-Napoca, Romania
Allel Hadjali, LIAS/ENSMA, Poitiers, France

Sung-Kook Han, Won Kwang University, South Korea
TzungaPei Hong, National University of Kaohsiung, Taiwan
Nikos Karacapilidis, University of Patras, Greece
Roula Karam, Università degli studi di Brescia, Italy
Hassan A. Karimi, University of Pittsburgh, USA
Sotirios Karetsos, Agricultural University of Athens, Greece
Fotis Kokkoras, TEI of Thessaly, Greece
Samad Kolahi, UNITEC, New Zealand
Nane Kratzke, Lübeck University of Applied Sciences, Germany
Anirban Kundu, Netaji Subhash Engineering College (under MAKAUT) / Computer Innovative Research Society, West Bengal, India
Sergio Luján-Mora, University of Alicante, Spain
Daniela Marghitu, Auburn University, USA
Edgard Marx, AKSW - University of Leipzig, Germany
Abdul-Rahman Mawlood-Yunis, Algonquin College, Canada
Michele Melchiori, Università degli Studi di Brescia, Italy
Héctor Menéndez, University College London, UK
Manfred Meyer, Westfälische Hochschule - University of Applied Sciences, Bocholt, Germany
Héctor F. Migallón Gomis, Universidad Miguel Hernández, Spain
Debajyoti Mukhopadhyay, Maharashtra Institute of Technology, India
Tope Omitola, University of Southampton, UK
Guadalupe Ortiz, University of Cadiz, Spain
Giuseppe Patane', CNR-IMATI, Italy
Agostino Poggi, DII - University of Parma, Italy
Prashant R. Nair, Amrita University, India
Talal H. Noor, Taibah University, Saudi Arabia
Tarmo Robal, Tallinn University of Technology, Estonia
Christophe Roche, Université Savoie Mont-Blanc, France
Marek Rychly, Brno University of Technology, Czech Republic
Demetrios Sampson, Curtin University, Australia
Sandra Sanchez-Gordon, Escuela Politécnica Nacional, Ecuador
Georgios Santipantakis, University of Piraeus, Greece
Hossein Sarrafzadeh, Unitec Institute of Technology, New Zealand
M. Sasikumar, CDAC Mumbai, India
Erich Schweighofer, University of Vienna - Centre for Computers and Law, Austria
Blerina Spahiu, University of Milano - Bicocca, Italy
Imon Banerjee, Stanford University School of Medicine, USA
Mariusz Trzaska, Polish-Japanese Academy of Information Technology, Poland
Domenico Ursino, University "Mediterranea" of Reggio Calabria, Italy
Taketoshi Ushiama, Kyushu University, Japan
Costas Vassilakis, University of the Peloponnese, Greece
Maurizio Vincini, Universita' di Modena e Reggio Emilia, Italy
Krzysztof Walczak, Poznan University of Economics, Poland
Toyohide Watanabe, Nagoya Industrial Science Research Institute, Japan
Jian Yu, Auckland University of Technology, New Zealand
Fouad Zablith, American University of Beirut, Lebanon
Yongfeng Zhang, University of Massachusetts Amherst, USA

Copyright Information

Discovering Geographical Patterns of Crime Localization in Mexico City

Roberto Zagal-Flores[1], Félix Mata-Rivera[2],
Instituto Politécnico Nacional,
UPIITA-IPN[1, 2]
Ciudad de México, México
e-mail: rzagalf@ipn.mx[1], mmatar@ipn.mx[2]

Christophe Claramunt[3], Edgar Catalan-Salgado[4]
Naval Academy Research Institute[3]
Brest Naval, 29240, France
Instituto Politécnico Nacional, ESCOM-IPN[4]
Ciudad de México, México
e-mail: claramunt@ecole-navale.fr[3], ecatalans@ipn.mx[4]

***Abstract*. The search for a better understanding of crime patterns in large urban areas is still a crucial issue that deserves novel research methods and approaches. In particular, combination of institutional databases and novel information medias such as social networks appear as a promising trend that might favor development of more efficient criminal information management and crime prevention systems. However, most existing systems do not take into account to the best of our knowledge the geographical dimension although this might provide a better representation of how crimes spread over space and time. The research presented in this paper develops a knowledge discovery approach based on a close integration of official, social and geographical data sources. The result is a modeling approach that provides a-priori knowledge of safe and unsafe places and the ones that are even candidates to become unsecured places. The aim is to not only give an overall geographical representation of crime patterns that might be useful for decision-makers, but also web-based resources to the citizens. The whole approach has been applied to Mexico City.**

Keywords-GKD; Crossing-data; Social Web mining; Geo-social Web Analytics; Web ontology.

I. INTRODUCTION

The research presented in this paper is grounded in the assumption that social networks offer novel resources to reflect population's opinion on insecurity problems occurring in urban zones. For instance, In Mexico City, people often denounce complaints, events, and unsafe places. Many Facebook pages and Twitter accounts also regularly report crimes that citizens suffer thus providing rich descriptions often located in space and timely stamped. Therefore, it clearly appears that if such crime data can be geographically analyzed, then it will be possible to build services to citizens and decision-aided systems to municipal authorities [20].

Over the past few years, many novel research approaches have been designed and developed based on social web mining and Geographic Knowledge Discovery (GKD) [5]) in order to solve novel challenges related to the integration of unstructured social data and structured data sources [23]. In fact not only these novel unstructured data sources require development of novel data integration and representation mechanisms, but also sound approaches to evaluate quality and veracity of the incoming data. It has been recently shown that quality and certainty of opinions and denunciations expressed on social networks can be increased when linked and related to additional data sources [5].

Crossing data would allow validating, confirming, or discovering non-intuitive knowledge at first sight (e.g., location and profile of the place or victim of a given crime). Therefore, external social data sources such as news websites, as these regularly report and discuss situations, events, or facts from different perspectives, can be combined with other web data sources to discover and search for geographical and temporal patterns.

On the other hand, news media might are likely to influence social perception of the insecurity problem as they occur in a given city. It has been particularly observed that for example social perception of insecurity in Mexico City has increased up to 69% [7], where 64.2% of the population reported that in the last three months, they modified their habits for fear of being a victim of a crime.

The research presented in this paper introduces a preliminary GKD social framework applied to crime data. The main contribution relies on the crossing of different datasets to discover some geographic and temporal crime patterns as reflected by social media, institutional data sources and the final public perception. The remainder of the paper is organized as follows. Section 2 outlines related work. Section 3 introduces the GKD social framework. Section 4 develops the data extraction while Section 5 presents the preprocessing process. Section 6 discusses the lessons learned from the analysis of crime data. The data crossing approach is presented in Section 7. Section 8 presents the preliminary results obtained and some evaluations. Finally, Section 9 draws the conclusions and outlines future work.

II. RELATED WORK

Studies on crime data have been conducted by many research domains such as spatial data mining, geographical analysis, Big Data analysis and crime prediction. For example, the work in [1] presents a collaborative community alert application that enables citizens to publish a complaint at the time a crime occurs, and to inform other users close to that area. In Mexico City, a web system regularly and interactively informs the state of insecurity in different neighborhoods [2]. A survey of crime prevention systems has been recently published and includes an analysis of the main web and mobile crime information systems, but so far there are no approaches that integrate unstructured social data and official data sources [19].

A series of spatial data mining approaches have been applied to the metropolitan area of Washington DC to discover and extract patterns from crime datasets [8] [9] [10}. A spatiotemporal-textual search engine and pattern discovery approach identify crime categories from collections of crime information [8]. The work developed in [9] provides a smart device-based Internet application to enable real-time location-based and search for crime incidents and reports. This system has the advantage of leveraging crowdsourced data to provide safe paths and crime analytics. The integrated framework proposed in [10] is also based on natural language processing whose objective is to extract, rank and score some crime events in space and time. Colocation analysis has been explored using geographical analysis and machine learning algorithms to identify and categorize regular patterns of crimes in some given locations [11]. For instance, the relationships between drink locations and habits (e.g., bars, alcohol, respectively) and crimes have been studies and show that crimes are often related to such behaviors. Next, the authors developed a neighborhood graph-based approach that searches for spatio-temporal patterns. A Geographical Information Systems (GIS) approach searches for criminal hot spots and drug cases in China [21]. Understanding the reasons behind crime patterns in space and time is also a domain of study that has been considered by machine learning algorithms, this is a crucial issue for crime prediction studies [18]. A crime analytics system based on temporal prediction analysis has been suggested in [22]. The authors developed a predictive system based on natural language processing, and whose objective is to identify the intensity of some crime events, using a combination with social-based data, public and private data.

Overall, and despite the novelty and interest of the above mentioned approach, most of them do not completely take advantage of the potential offered by a combination of crime, social and spatio-temporal data. We believe that such integration should provide novel means for discovering new geographical and temporal patterns, as well as an evaluation of the degree of certainty associated to such trends. The research presented in this paper proposes a hybrid semantic approach that considers such challenges, and combines and crosses social and official crime data using ontology exploration and machine learning techniques.

III. THE GKD SOCIAL FRAMEWORK

The GKD social framework is fed from official and unofficial sources, data from the national public security system [16], verified user publications, Facebook and Twitter communities, as well as news web pages.

The information collected refers to descriptions of criminal events and complaints, which will be analyzed and displayed on a crime map. The goal is to characterize crime from a geographical perspective. What characteristics describe a crime place? What is the geographic and spatial profile of a crime place? How often does a crime occur in a particular place? What places can become a potential place where a crime can happen? The geographic information is provided by collaborative maps and official cartography from the local government.

Our approach adapts knowledge discovery in databases (KDD) methodology, which refers to the non-trivial process of discovering knowledge and potentially useful information within the data contained in some information repository [2]. Our framework uses four phases: 1) retrieval and extraction of data related to crime, events, and social complaints by geographical areas from Facebook and Twitter, news web pages, and official data sources; 2) semantic analysis of data using crime web ontology; 3) classification, which considers supervised machine learning techniques to separate the crime activity and geographic patterns; and 4) crossing geographic patterns and official data to acquire new knowledge and evaluate the certainty of social data. Finally, the main principles of our approach are illustrated in Figure 1 and are part of a previous work [5].

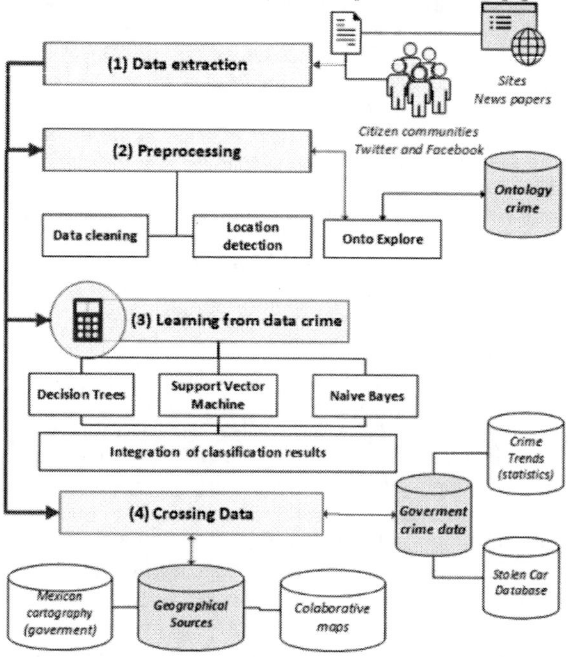

Figure 1. A GKD Social Framework for Crime Data

Figure 1 shows the main phases of our approach; the GKD is the combination of the semantic analysis and machine learning layers. The first layer uses the ontology to pre-classify all the unstructured data obtained from the web and social networks. The second layer makes the classifications for official and social data (it means structured and unstructured data). The following subsections will explain each one of these phases:

IV. DATA EXTRACTION

The extraction process consists of retrieving the reports of complaints from official sources (a fragment of the information can be seen in Figure 2) and unofficial sources (see a sample of publication in Figure 3).

	ENTIDA	MUNICIPIO	MODALIDAD	TIPO	SUBTIPO	ENERO	FEBRERO
2011	MEXICO	TECAMAC	DELITOS PATRIMC	ABUSO DE CONFI	ABUSO DE CONFIANZA	9	5
2011	MEXICO	TECAMAC	DELITOS PATRIMC	DAÑO EN PROPIE	DAÑO EN PROPIEDAD AJENA	34	32
2011	MEXICO	TECAMAC	DELITOS PATRIMC	EXTORSION	EXTORSION		
2011	MEXICO	TECAMAC	DELITOS PATRIMC	FRAUDE	FRAUDE	2	1
2011	MEXICO	TECAMAC	DELITOS PATRIMC	DESPOJO	CON VIOLENCIA		
2011	MEXICO	TECAMAC	DELITOS PATRIMC	DESPOJO	SIN VIOLENCIA		
2011	MEXICO	TECAMAC	DELITOS PATRIMC	DESPOJO	SIN DATOS	9	7

Figure 2. Data from National Public Security System (data in Spanish)

In the case of Figure 2, complaint data were obtained from [2], and it contains fields, such as municipality (location of the crime), type of crime, subtype of crime, and date. Figure 3 shows a post (in Spanish) retrieved from a Facebook community specializing in citizens' reports of crimes called "Ecatepec on alert" (text in Spanish « Ecatepec en Alerta»). Ecatepec is a municipality (in the country of Mexico) with high crime rates, and it is located near Mexico City.

Regarding the number of crime complaints dataset in official and unofficial sources, a Facebook page named "Ecatepec denunciation" (in Spanish « Denuncia Ecatepec ») extracted 6771 posts of complaints. In opposite, the news web page named "A Fondo Estado de Mexico" (site of news crime) only extracted 100 datasets from complaints.

Ecatepec Alerta
3 horas

"me robaron mi motoneta hoy a las 3 am por la curva del diablo las placas son 8N6VZ . Fue en la estación del Méxibus Adolfo Lopez Mateos"

Translation: Ecatepec on alert, "My motorcycle was stolen today at 3 am at the Devil's Curve. The numberplate is 8N6VZ. It was at the Méxibus in Adolfo Lopez Mateos station."

Figure 3. Nonofficial information from Facebook (post in Spanish)

V. PREPROCESSING

The data extracted is processed with a computational linguistic process whereby the text is cleaned and converted to lower case, words are lemmatized, and punctuation marks and emoticons are eliminated. An example in Figure 4 shows an original post from Facebook about a complaint, then below shows the result processed linguistically.

Denuncia Ecatepec
19 de noviembre a las 21:16

#AutoRobado
Hola Denuncia El día de ayer 18 de Noviembre a las 7:35pm fui víctima de asalto a mano armada en valle de aragon primera sección me quitaron un carro Versa modelo 2016 con placas MZG-4071 color gris plata si alguien tiene informes les agradecería me lo hagan saber por este medio
Gracias

Lemmatization: autorobado denunciar dia ayer 18 noviembre 7 35 pm victima asalta mano armada valle de aragon primero seccion quitar carro versa modelo 2016 placa mzg 4071 color grises plata informa agradecer hacer medio

Translation: Complaint Ecatepec, #StolenAuto "Hello Complaint Ecatepec, yesterday November 18 at 7:35 p.m. I was the victim of an armed robbery in the Valley of Aragon first section. A car Nissan Versa model 2016 was stolen. The numberplate is MZG-4071, and the color is gray silver. If anyone has reports, I would be grateful."

Output: "StolenAuto report day yesterday 18 november 7 35 pm victim assault armed hand valley of Aragon first section car Nissan versa model 2016 plate mzg 4071 color gray silver informs thank to do medium"

Figure 4. Lemmatization of a Facebook post

A. Location analysis

Once the data is cleaned and processed, the following phase consists of determining the location where the event occurred. It is limited only to data containing terms, words, or names of places. The process uses GeoNames [17], gazetteers, and a terms dictionary. This phase comprises three steps:

1. The first step consists of identifying all place names within the data and it is achieved using a prebuilt specialized terms dictionary. It ensures that the tweet, post, or data from the web page describes a geographical place (the data that cannot be identified are discarded.)
2. The second step disambiguates the possible names for the same geographic location but with different granularity (municipality, colony, street, and avenue). Then, the GeoNames web service [17] is used to determine the granularity of the place.
3. In the third step, a gazetteer is used to identify place names and synonyms within a particular area. Figure 5 shows an example of this analysis.

```
Ecatepec -> a geographical location
Ecatepec of Morelos -> a geographical location
Ecatepec of Morelos -> a synonym: Ecatepec
Ecatepec -> a part of the State of Mexico
```

Figure 5. Location Analysis

The location analysis is an experimental phase. Hence, it can be enhanced by machine learning methods [4].

B. Semantic analysis

This process focuses on social network data and web pages. The analysis consists of pre-classifying the data to determine to which category the security domain belong to (e.g., security, theft, complaint) by using an ontology prebuilt based on concepts derived from security domain. In particular, the ontology helps to determine if the data describes a crime, complaint, or they are part of another context. The algorithm OntoClassifier is shown as follows.

OntoClassifier Algorithm

```
1. Begin
2. Let q[i] elements of user query
3. N = 0
4.   while n < i
5.    parsing and identification (q[i])
6.    node.start()
7.      while node != null
8.       j++, i++
9.       if similarity(concept_name)
          conVec[j]neighborhood_relations(node)
          node.next()
10.       geoVector[k] = geographic_search(conVec[j])
11.     thematic_and_social_search(conVec[j])
12.     temporal_search(conVec[j])
13.    j++, k++, n++
14. End
```

The algorithm works as follows: the input is the data extracted from social media and web pages; then, the ontology is explored using the algorithm OntoClassifier (adapted from [3]). Each term identified by the social media source is correlated with the Ontology. If a match occurs, the context of the concept (all neighborhood concepts) is extracted, and they are stored into a vector (Algorithm 1, lines from 4 to 10). The vector is used to determine which domain and category the data belongs; it is known by using the hyperonym relation of the ontology. This relation indicates the domain and category. In that way, the output obtained is a pre-classification of data showing what type of crime is described or mentioned in the data by using three parameters: time, thematic, and location components. The classification is based on the scale of categories used in [2]. An example of the output appears in Figure 5 where a console screenshot is shown after the OntoClassifier program is executed and the matching is listed.

```
Robar motoneta → Delito tipo Robo de auto
3 am → Hora
Placa → Atributo con valor → 8n6vz
```

Translation:"
Steal motorcycle -> Auto theft -> type of crime,
3 am -> Time,
Plate -> Attribute with value -> 8n6vz"

Figure 6. Post pre-classification process

As Figure 6 shows a pre-classified post, in the first line (in Spanish) the term "Steal scooter" is pre-classified as a crime; "Theft." In the second line, the text "3 am" is classified as a time component. In the third line, the term "vehicle registration plate" is classified as a value attribute, and finally, the numeric value "8n6vz" is extracted.

The ontology was designed based on the methodology suggested in [6] and the concepts that are used more often in social networks. A brief extract of the ontology is shown in Figure 7. The ontology describes the nature of the crime context in Mexico City.

Figure 7. Crime Ontology (fragment)

In addition to this process, a data dictionary is based on a taxonomy that was built using the data from Statistical Classification of Crimes (CED, by the acronym in Spanish). The CED offers classification in three categories: crimes against people, crimes against society, and crimes against the state (they are available at [24]). The taxonomy is applied as a refinement process in the classification of crime type using the OntoClassifier on the data.

VI. LEARNING FROM DATA CRIME

In this stage, characterization is processed and the data is classified using machine learning methods. The main goal of the classification is to get the separation of the crime activity and geographical profile. The characterization is performed by using three classification algorithms: *C5.0 Decision Tree (DT), Naive Bayes (NB), and Support Vector Machine (SVM)*. These algorithms have been applied in previous approaches like [4][12] and represent a layer of supervised learning. In this stage, when a pre-processed crime document (from social networks or web sources) is assigned to a crime class (e.g., carjacking category), two of the three classifiers has to match in the same class. In the case that the three algorithms assign the same object to different classes, the *SVM* result is chosen because this classifier has a better performance according to our tests.

The classification process is executed twice (each execution uses *TD, NB and SVM*):

Classification by crime profile: This is the categorization of a new document into a specific class of crime, such as carjacking, assault on passersby, and kidnapping. To improve the visualization of discovered results, a sub-process detects and highlights relevant words inside a classified document, for example, gun, knife, car, violence, thieves (persons, guys), schedule (night, day, morning, time stamp). This sub-process uses a bag of crime words (based on a weighted selection of concepts from our ontology) and considers the lexical and grammatical information of the classified document [13].

Classification by geographical area: in the previous pre-processing phase, a location analysis was developed to obtain a general location (e.g., state or municipality). However, it is necessary to classify the specific location; this allows a correlation between crimes, crowdsourcing complaints, and localities. The classes are known places in municipalities or states: popular zones, tourist sites, buildings, and others.

Finally, the cross-validation is used to estimate how accurate a predictive algorithm will be in practice. In K-fold cross-validation, the sample data are divided into K subsets. One of the subsets is used as test data, and the rest (K-1) as training data. This ensures that the classifications are independent of the partition between training and test data. The preliminary results of K-fold cross-validation show that the SVM algorithm maintains an average accuracy of 87 percent. The DT and SVM algorithms have a performance of around 78.77 percent. However, for small data, NB develops a higher performance than the other two classifiers [4].

Finally, the WEKA software [25] was used to test the performance of the classifiers and make an analysis of the output obtained.

VII. CROSSING DATA

After identifying the "type of crime," it is possible to correlate this information with other data sources to discover unexpected knowledge. For example, a post extracted from Facebook that belongs to the "carjacking" class and whose text contains the plate number, the framework can use the official database of stolen vehicles (vehicle information system of the Mexican government) [14] and search the number of the "vehicle registration plate." If that number exists, one can conclude whether the car was stolen or not and discover the level of certainty of the information extracted.

Besides using official [15] and collaborative maps, one can discover additional geographical relations around the crime locations. For example, the post with the text "A Honda Civic car was stolen violently near to 'Parque Lindavista' mall by three armed men wearing sports clothes at 9 p.m" (by crime profile, the post is classified as "carjacking" class). "Parque Lindavista" is a known mall of the Delegation Gustavo A. Madero in Mexico City (geographically, the post was classified in the "popular zone" class) and there are hospitals around the mall (crossing with official maps). We discover that carjacking occurs in desolate urban areas. Another observation is that this crime happens in Ecatepec municipality (in the State of Mexico, Mexico) in similar conditions to Delegation Gustavo A. Madero: at night, by two or three armed men, and in desolate zones.

Other patterns regarding carjacking are the number of individuals who are committing this crime (in this case, two or three persons), the use of cars without a number registration plate, and the co-occurrence of crimes like drug trafficking and carjacking. According to the official data, carjacking happens regularly in Mexico City and in the country of Mexico.

VIII. PRELIMINARY RESULTS AND DATA VISUALIZATION

This section outlines and shows the preliminary results of the experiments made in the city of Mexico. The input data includes around 105,036 users, 1,396,408 datasets from Twitter, 25,360 posts from Facebook, and 150,000 from news web pages. The following attributes were considered in the dataset: type of crime, year, month and number of complaints, places where it occurred, the number of users and sources used.

In Figure 8, the areas with a similar unsafe geographical profile are represented in red.

Figure 8. Zones with similar unsafe geographical profile (Mexico City)

While Figure 9 shows a prototype user interface for data visualization and patterns discovery, crimes are also clustered in categories and key terms.

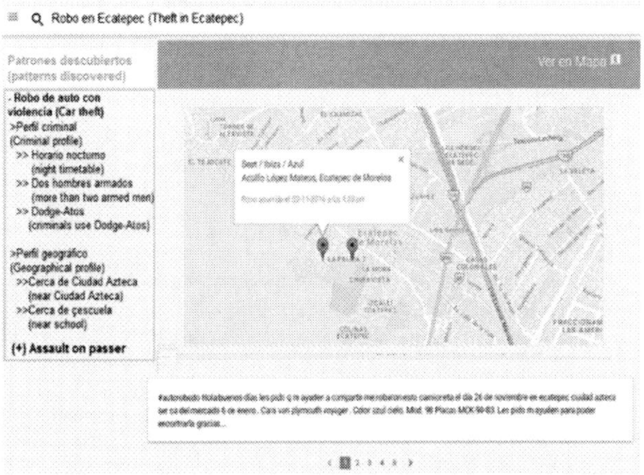

Figure 9. User interface for visualization of geographic patterns

Figure 10 shows how the carjacking crime behaves in the last seven years in the first six months and different geographic places.

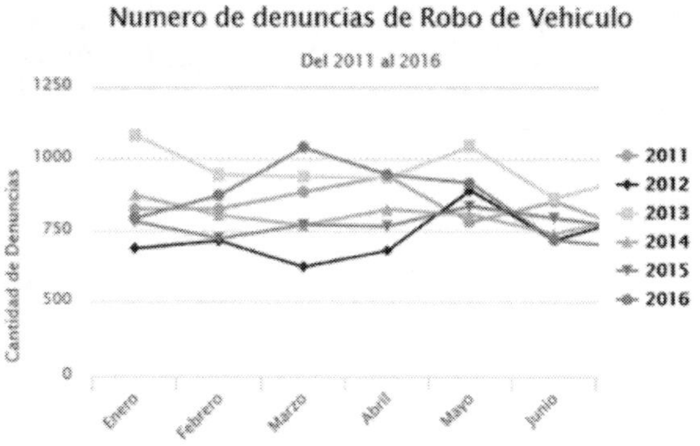

Figure 10. Behavior of crimes in unsafe geographic profiles

Figure 9 and Figure 10 show the integration of official and social media data.

IX. CONCLUSIONS

The preliminary research presented in this paper introduces a GKD approach that combines Semantic and Machine Learning techniques, data correlations applied to discover patterns and the emerging levels of data certainty. The preliminary results identify and show the geographical profiles of unsafe places, patterns, and crime behaviors in different geographical areas.

Future work will consider additional classification experiments and depped learning methods using different crime data sources. At the interface level, we plan to develop some user-oriented interfaces designed with usability principles, advanced data visualization, experiments using Stanford API, and mobile applications development.

ACKNOWLEDGMENT

The authors of this paper thank God, CONACYT project number 1051, the Laboratorio de Cómputo Móvil-UPIITA, COFAA-IPN, SIP-IPN project 20171086, and Instituto Politécnico Nacional (IPN) for their support.

REFERENCES

[1] Semaforo.com.mx. (2017). NGO Crime and Safety Report. [Online] Available at: http://www.semaforo.com.mx/ [Accessed 1 Apr. 2017].

[2] Webmining.cl. (2017). KDD Knowledge Discovery in Databases | WebMining. [online] Available at: http://www.webmining.cl/2011/01/proceso-de-extraccion-de-conocimiento/ [Accessed 1 Apr. 2017].

[3] F. Mata, and C. Claramunt, GeoST: geographic, thematic and temporal information retrieval from heterogeneous web data sources. In Web and Wireless Geographical Information Systems (pp. 5-20). Springer Berlin Heidelberg, 2011.

[4] A. Sampson, Comparing classification algorithms in data mining, Master of Science, Central Connecticut State University, 2016.

[5] R. Zagal-Flores, M. Mata, and C. Claramunt, Geographical Knowledge Discovery applied to the Social Perception of Pollution in the City of Mexico. 9th ACM SIGSPATIAL International Workshop on Location-Based Social Networks. San Francisco, California, USA.

[6] M. Corcho, et al., Methodologies tools and languages for building ontologies. Where is their meeting point? Universidad Politécnica de Madrid, Campus de Montegancedo s/n, Madrid 28660, España, 2001.

[7] C. Jasso López, "Perception of Insecurity in Mexico", Mexican Journal of Public Opinion, Volume 15, July–December 2013, Pages 12-29, ISSN 1870-7300.

[8] X. Liu, C. Jian, and C. Tien Lu, A spatio-temporal-textual crime search engine. In Proceedings of the 18th SIGSPATIAL International Conference on Advances in Geographic Information Systems (GIS '10). ACM, New York (2010), NY, USA, 528-529.

[9] S. Shah, F. Bao, C. Lu, I. Chen. CROWDSAFE: Crowd Sourcing of Crime Incidents and Safe Routing on Mobile Devices (Demo Paper). ACM SIGSPATIAL GIS'11, November 1-4, 2011. Chicago, IL, USA. ACM, ISBN 978-1-4503-1031-4/11/11.

[10] B. Wang, et al.., An integrated framework for spatio-temporal-textual search and mining. In Proceedings of the 20th International Conference on Advances in Geographic Information Systems (2012), New York, NY, USA, 570-573.

[11] P. Mohan, et al., A neighborhood graph based approach to regional co-location pattern discovery: a summary of results. In Proceedings of the 19th ACM SIGSPATIAL International Conference on Advances in Geographic Information Systems (GIS '11)

[12] J. Han, J. Pei, and M. Kamber, Data Mining: Concepts and Techniques. Elsevier, Jun 9, 2011 - 744 pages.

[13] G. Sidorov, "Should Syntactic N-grams Contain Names of Syntactic Relations?". International Journal of Computational Linguistics and Applications, Vol. 5, No. 1, 2014, pp. 139–158.

[14] www2.repuve.gob.mx. (2017). *Consulta Ciudadana*. [online] Available at: http://www2.repuve.gob.mx:8080/ciudadania/ [Accessed 1 Apr. 2017].

[15] inegi.org.mx. (2017). [online] Available at: http://www.inegi.org.mx/geo/contenidos/mapadigital/ [Accessed 1 Apr. 2017].

[16] Secretariadoejecutivo.gob.mx. (2017). Secretariado Ejecutivo :: Inicio. [online] Available at: http://www.secretariadoejecutivo.gob.mx [Accessed 1 Apr. 2017].

[17] Geonames.org. (2017). Geonames. [online] Available at: http://www.geonames.org [Accessed 17 Apr. 2017].

[18] 18. C.-H. Yu, W. Ding, P. Chen, and M. Morabito, "Crime forecasting using spatio-temporal pattern with ensemble learning," in Advances in Knowledge Discovery and Data Mining: 18th Pacific-Asia Conference, PAKDD 2014, Tainan, Taiwan, May 13–16, 2014. Proceedings, Lecture Notes in Computer Science, pp. 174–185.

[19] 19. T. Moon, S. Heo and S. Lee, Ubiquitous Crime Prevention System (UCPS) for a Safer City, Procedia Environmental Sciences, Open Access Journal Volume 22, 2014, ISSN 1878-0296.

[20] J. Ratcliffe, "Crime mapping: spatial and temporal challenges," in Handbook of Quantitative Criminology, pp. 5–24, Springer, New York, NY, USA, 2010

[21] L. Lei, The GIS-based Research on Criminal Cases Hotspots Identifying, Procedia Environmental Sciences, Open Access Journal, Volume 12, 2012, Pages 957-963, ISSN 1878-0296,

[22] Hitachi Data Systems unveils new advancements in predictive policing to support safer, smart societies." Mena Report, 29/08/2015.

[23] F. Mata, et al., "A Mobile Information System Based on Crowd-Sensed and Official Crime Data for Finding Safe Routes: A Case Study of Mexico City," Mobile Information Systems, vol. 2016, Article ID 8068209, 11 pages, 2016. doi:10.1155/2016/806

[24] www3.inegi.org.mx. (2017). Clasificación Estadística de Delitos (CED). [online] Available at: http://www3.inegi.org.mx/sistemas/clasificaciones/delitos.aspx [Accessed 10 Jan. 2017].

[25] cs.waikato.ac.nz. (2017). Weka 3 - Data Mining with Open Source Machine Learning Software in Java. [online] Available at: http://www.cs.waikato.ac.nz/ml/weka/ [Accessed 10 Jan. 2017

Ontology Based Aspect Oriented Opinion Summary Methodology

Dervis Kanbur
Kuveyt Turk R.D. Service,
Department of Computer Engineering
Yildiz Technical University
Istanbul, Turkey
E-mail: dervis.kanbur@std.yildiz.edu.tr

Mehmet S. Aktas
Department of Computer Engineering
Yildiz Technical University
Istanbul, Turkey
E-mail: mehmet@ce.yildiz.edu.tr

Abstract— **Enterprises selling over the web generally request feedbacks from customers on their purchased products/services. Thanks to e-commerce in an increasingly developing structure, the number of customer feedbacks grows rapidly. Due to the great increase in the number of e-commerce enterprises and customers, it becomes difficult for a potential customer to read these feedbacks while making decisions. It becomes almost impossible for the producer to monitor these feedbacks as well. Product feature extraction from customer reviews is an important operation in opinion mining. The extracted features help to assess the opinions written by customers who have purchased specific products and they provide opinions of customers regarding their positive/negative experiences. Because most of the customer reviews are asyntactic plain texts, methods should be developed for extraction of implicit and explicit product features expressed in customer reviews and comments. In this research, we aim to develop a methodology that examines the opinions, thoughts and comments, written in Turkish, about the products and summarizes the features of the products and the emotional processes related to these properties. Our study differs from others in that product characteristics expressed using synonyms or word groups can be identified, and features can be detected with greater accuracy using ontologies that include product specifications. Our study offers successful results in product feature extraction. Experimental work on opinion/idea/comment for some products on e-commerce sites shows that our methodology yields positive results.**

Keywords-text mining; sentiment classification; review summarizing; synonym word group; ontology;

I. INTRODUCTION

In the developing and globalizing world, measuring and evaluating customer satisfaction for organizations operating in the trade field and using this information to improve customer experience has become a key to gain advantage in today's competitive market. Thus, organizations that develop new products / services or market improved products / services will be able to effectively increase service qualities, capture customer trust and reach a stable customer portfolio in product usage.

Because the number of skilled workers is likely disproportional to the workload, the number of customers and products in today's commercial enterprises, monitoring customer satisfaction becomes quite difficult/impossible. The features such as obtaining written opinions/suggestions of customers on products over the Internet, rapid analysis of these data and assessments on products with minimum human resources in a fast way, shall free the way of doing business actively and developing products according to customers' requests for enterprises and enable maximum customer satisfaction.

With the development of technology from the other side, the rapid development of the virtual store network increases the number of online shopping and the variety of products sold. Through the virtual shopping world, the need for comments of customers who have purchased the same product before has become prevalent. Nevertheless, customers become used to writing feedbacks for products they purchase. As a result, thereof, products with more comments indicate an increased popularity. Thus, some products collect more comments. Hundreds of comments on these products from different sources (in other words, different e-commerce sites) make it difficult to assess the general satisfaction degree of customers browsing through these comments. It is not possible to make a general deduction for customers who read a part of these comments.

At the early undeveloped stages of data handling, we observe that data analysis reveals the competitive aspects of firms. As time passed, the competitors acquiring these capabilities have removed this advantage. So, for today's enterprises, development of more complex data analysis approaches become obligatory, in order to get a step ahead. To help marketing people get ahead safely in this challenging competition environment, an independently sponsored research unit, Harvard Business Review Analytic Services [7] within the Harvard Business Review Group has researched how leading marketing enterprises integrated customer and marketing data and how they used it to increase their companies' performance. This research has revealed that the data source used for customers and marketing activities were the most important element in competition.

As the Internet world grows up and social media is used more frequently, it becomes possible to take customer reviews through various channels. It is essential to respond positively to customer needs in sales & marketing. Monitoring and responding to these needs shall help companies in reaching maximum customer satisfaction and provide an improvement of marketing data at a significant rate. In this case, the need for an application capable of being implemented rapidly and easily by companies, analyzing customer reviews, performing certain deductions on the product according to the analysis is among the reason motivating our research.

The aim of this research is to increase the quality of products/services in line with feedbacks of customers and ensure customer satisfaction within the product sales and service sector and to develop a methodology for creating mutual satisfaction through win-win strategy. The method we propose in this research shall collect customers' feedbacks dynamically, make deductions on product features by analyzing the reviews, and enable figuring out the positive/negative aspects of products.

A. *Research Questions*

In order to achieve the motivation mentioned above, the research questions we have determined are as follows:

1) R.Q-1: What should be a method that can process customer comments for products sold on the Internet and automatically extract the properties of the products and then summarize the positive or negative opinions of the customers based on their product characteristics? How should the architecture of the software that implements such a method be and how can it be developed?

2) R.Q-2: How should a methodology be developed that will reveal whether the product features revealed by the analysis of the data obtained from the customer comments are the actual product characteristics?

B. *Contribution of Research*

The increase in online resources where different ideas/opinions/comments are shared, and the fact that these shares are in different formats, reveals the need to develop methods to collect data. Within the scope of this research, a web crawler application has been developed to find, download, parse, and collect customer comments (texts containing comments/ideas/ thoughts) in such sources. In order to extract product features from collected customer comments and to perform feature based sentiment analysis, the following functions have been implemented in order: (1) Extracting product features from Turkish comments, (2) To determine whether each feature is used with the word group that contains positive or negative expression according to Turkish grammar rules (3) Identifying Product features, identified with different words but with the same meaning, and combining under one feature title (4) taking advantage of ontology, comparing actual product properties with determined properties (5) summarizing sentiment analysis results. In the scope of this research, a methodology which can determine the properties of products from the interpretations entered by the customers and can analyze the emotions related to these properties is proposed. A prototype implementation of the developed methodology has been developed and the success of the methodology has been demonstrated through experimental work on the prototype.

C. *Organizational Structure*

In the Introduction, we talked about our motivation to trigger this research. The main issues related to our similar researches and researches are summarized in literature review. In the part "Proposed Software Architecture", we talked about our methodology for analyzing customer comments and determining product characteristics. In the part "Development", how the methodology used in the system developed in the research is realized is explained. In Section IV, the success of the proposed methodology is examined. In Section V, the results we have obtained after conducting the research are discussed.

II. LITERATURE REVIEW AND BASIS TOPICS

In this part, we will discuss the studies performed on extracting product feature from customer reviews. Generally, these studies are sorted into different classes as frequency based approach [1], statistical approach [11], and relational based approach [2]. Since the methodology we provide in this research is in the frequency-based approach category, we concentrate on studies in this area especially if we do not review the literature. The most prominent work in this category is the method proposed by Hu and Liu, which extracts the most frequent terms from the reviews as product features [1]. In this research, It was assumed that the product features shall be expressed clearly by nouns or noun phrases in the sentence. Association Rule Mining was implemented to find frequently repeated words. When the frequently repeating features' list is generated, all words expressing an opinion around these features are figured out. The main disadvantage of this method is that some words that are not actually product features may be extracted as a feature because they are used frequently. After identifying the features in the texts, it is necessary to reveal the opinions associated with these features. The works done in this area is categorized as opinion mining. In opinion mining studies focuses on the following processes:

A. *Subjective Classification*

In this category of studies, a given text/sentence is searched if it contains any opinion [1] [12]. These studies consider whether a sentence contains a positive or negative opinion rather than the general document.

B. *Sentiment Classification*

It is the process of trying to find out whether a given sentence is positive/negative or neutral. In this category, sentiment based classification studies are inspired by cognitive linguistics [13]. In some studies, the texts were classified with certain specific sentimental words [14]. In these researches, each word was added to a dictionary and it was marked to detect if it has a positive/negative expression. The statistics found using a search engine in a study, which was developed for common languages such as English and an effective study, which uses WordNet, were matched with words and documents and a learning technique was generated [8]. In some studies, sentiment classifications were performed using machine learning techniques [9]. The other studies in this area have not been designed to give knowledge of which opinions indicate which feature.

C. *Opinion Summarizing*

It is a function that is worked on to express multiple opinions or a long opinion text in a short way. Several summarizing techniques basically work on two categories. Creating templates and extracting passages. Most studies in this area were developed in a single document. Whereas some studies were performed on multiple documents containing the same information in order to search for similarities and differences [10].

Our study was performed on Turkish reviews and different words, abbreviations or loan word groups are checked through an available list and the recall value is being increased by combining words which were extracted as different features. It is distinguished from previous studies in its being performed on Turkish reviews, assessment of loan words, and detecting synonyms.

The study we have proposed in this paper is based on Turkish interpretations and allows us to extract more accurate features by combining different word, abbreviation or foreign word groups which express the same feature (in other words, the words that are expressed as different features but which express the same feature). By using field ontologies, it is checked whether the determined properties are met in ontology. Our developed feature extraction method is separated from existing studies by being able to determine on the basis of Turkish interpretations, use of ontologies and synonyms and to collect them under the same heading.

Product features are extracted from multiple customer reviews in our work. In this respect, it differs from the traditional text summarization. A method that works on multiple comments / text clusters instead of a single text has been developed. Our goal here is to extract product features on multiple texts, rather than finding similarities or differences in texts. Again, within the scope of our study, a list of words and phrases for adjectives with positive or negative meaning in the Turkish language was extracted and their sentiment ratings were determined. In our study, sentiment analysis was done at the sentence level, not at the document level. By using the sentimental adjectives in the sentences, positive or negative opinions related to the product features in the sentence were determined.

III. THE PROPOSED METHODLOGY

The details of our methodology given in Figure 1 are given below. The Turkish Feature Identification System works on data (eg: e-commerce site selling X Television Brand, the source of X product) obtained by finding, gathering, decomposing comment texts of a product with a specific source. These data may be obtained from a single source where the product is sold, or it can occur in different environments if the product is sold in more than one source (e-commerce site). These environments may be sampled as e-commerce websites, social media groups, opinion expressing websites. As shown in Figure 1 the study was performed on data acquired from selected e-commerce and opinion expressing web sites. The system is designed to be used for analysis and reporting of customer reviews by integrating it to these web sites. Through the integration of this system with companies' e-commerce websites, it would be possible to observe how the product generates opinions from performed reviews. This would increase the customer satisfaction and contribute positively to the product marketing.

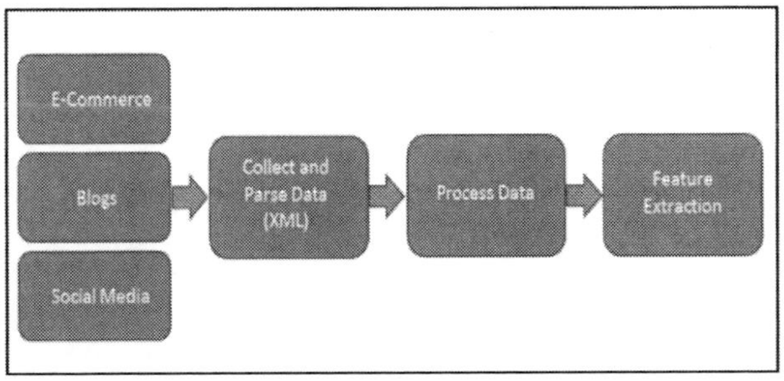

Figure 1. The Proposed Methodoloy Workflow

A. *Data Collection*

In this phase, texts containing comments/ideas/opinions are obtained in the data source. Within the scope of this research, because of the difficulty in finding a ready dataset prepared in Turkish, reviews from two selected websites (arabainceleme.com, hepsiburada.com) were extracted and prepared for processing. However, since the method we propose is extensible, it can be integrated into the system from other data sources so that it can provide output in the format the system expects.

B. *Data Pre-Processing*

In our study, some preprocessing techniques were used. Primarily, stop words likely to recur in reviews, which are required by the language, were cleared. Then, the roots of words were obtained by stemming on the words which made the texts containing comments/opinions/ideas. Within the scope of word rooting function, because some words from the Turkish language had the same roots, there was a problem of not to be able to pick the right structure in stemming. In such cases, the next words were examined and formation of a combined structure was checked.

For example, a sentence including the expression "kullanım kılavuzu(user manual)" may be given as an example of this problem. When we observe the stem of the word "kullanım", the verb "kullan" appears. But its suffix "ım" indicates that this word may be used as a noun. In such words, the following word was examined to recognize its type. Because the word "kılavuzu" has a noun root and it has a noun generating suffix "u", the previous word "kullanım" was assumed as a noun. In following parts of the contribution, the algorithm which discovers Turkish compound words shall be explained in detail.

C. *Extracting Feature From Data*

In the process of extracting features from data, the Zemberek Natural Language Processing library was used [15]. An ontology related to the product features was created by making use of the data dictionary of the Turkish Language Association. Classification Based on Associations

(CBA) algorithm was used to find the frequency of the words in the obtained sentences. Recall and Precision metrics were used to measure the obtained values. The process of extracting properties is made up of the following sub-steps: word tagging, compound word detection, extraction of frequently repetitive product features, extraction of opinion words, extraction of opinion sentence tendencies, and combination of related words. We explain these sub-steps in detail below.

1) Word Tagging

After the removal of stop words, we have tagged the remaining words. Figure 2 shows a tagged sentence after the process.

The example sentence in Figure 2 is as follows: "Tam ihtiyaçlarıma göre bir araç, düşük viteslerde gaza biraz yüklenmek gerekiyor ama hızını aldıktan sonra gerçekten etkileyici (the car design as my needs, in low gears the needs to load to gas a bit, but it's really impressive)". For each sentence in the comment contained in each comment text, an identifier is assigned to each word, and the tagged data are recorded in XML as shown in Figure 2.

```
<Tag>ADJECTIVE</Tag>Tam</Text>
<Tag>NOUN</Tag><Text>ihtiyaçlarıma</Text>
<Tag>PREPOSITION</Tag><Text>göre</Text>
<Tag>NUMERAL</Tag><Text>bir</Text>
<Tag>NOUN</Tag><Text>araç</Text>
<Tag>NOUN</Tag><Text>düşük</Text>
<Tag>NOUN</Tag><Text>viteslerde</Text>
<Tag>NOUN</Tag><Text>gaza</Text>
<Tag>NOUN</Tag><Text>biraz</Text>
<Tag>VERB</Tag><Text>yüklenmek</Text>
<Tag>VERB</Tag><Text>gerekiyor</Text>
<Tag>NOUN</Tag><Text>ama</Text>
<Tag>NOUN</Tag><Text>hızını</Text>
<Tag>VERB</Tag><Text>aldıktan</Text>
<Tag>TIME</Tag><Text>sonra</Text>
<Tag>ADJECTIVE</Tag><Text>gerçekten</Text>
<Tag>ADJECTIVE</Tag><Text>etkileyici</Text>
```

Figure 2. Example of Tagging Sentence

2) Turkish Compound Word Detection

In our implemented word tagging structure, the word's structure is extracted in relation to its stem. However, some features of the products may be expressed phrases constructed from noun phrases, adjective clauses, loan words and different compound words. Detection of these structures was determined within the scope of this study. A compound word detection algorithm specifically developed for Turkish language is shown in Figure 3. Within the context of this study, it is assumed that the words that express opinions are adjectives. However, considering that a product feature can also be expressed by adjective phrases, the adjectives used in such a case are considered to be part of the word groups expressing the product characteristic, and no sentiment analysis is performed on the adjectives in this case.

a) Detection of Various Structures from the Same Stem

In the tagging process, data root detection is performed by stemming on the word. However, detection of real tags of words in two different structures with roots having the same letters has appeared as a problem in front of us. We have tried to tag these words with multiple structures by combining them with following words.

For example; "gaz pedalı çok hafif" and "araç gaz ile çalışırken performansı düşüyor", the word "gaz" in the sentences has a different meaning in each term. While the "gas pedal" word group is a name proposition in the first sentence, the other sentence does not have such a formation. For this reason, it is necessary to correctly determine in what sense the word is used in order analyze the sentences correctly. In order to distinguish the words in this situation, we proposed a compound word detection algorithm as shown in Figure 3.

In the given algorithm detail, the sequential operations are as follows:

The block between lines 4-45 processes words in the given sentence.

The block between lines 5-25 handles the cases in which the word root is a noun. In this case:

- If the next word has got a noun-phrase suffix
- If the next word has got one of the nouns –den and –in suffixes
- If the next word is a verb and has got one of the –me (passive voice) -im -in suffixes
- If the word has got noun-phrase -ın suffix
- If the word has got a possession suffix –lı or absence suffix –sız
- If the word has got a noun –de suffix and if the previous word is verb

if the word has one of these conditions, it is deduced that "this word may be part of the combined word".

The block between lines 26-44, handles the cases when the word root is a verb. In this case:

- If the word has got only one suffix and the next word is an adjective
- If one the suffixes of the word is a negation suffix, and the next word is a noun and has got a noun-phrase –ı suffix.
- If the word has got two suffixes and one of them is necessarily an –erek suffix and the previous word is a noun.
- If the word has got two suffixes and one of them is –dik –en or –im, and the next word is a noun and has one of the noun-phrase suffixes –ı –ın –de.

if the word has one of these conditions, it is deduced that "this word may be part of the combined word".

In line 45, if the word is marked as a compound word, it is added to the compound word list.

Lines 50-70 deal with the words on the compound word list. If a word / word group has the following conditions, this word / word group is combined with the next word itself.

- If it is not compound and is a noun and is nominative case

- If it is not compound and has got a noun-phase suffix –ın

```
Procedure PhraseDetector
List phrasedList=new List;
for each word in sentence{
 isPhrased=false;
 if word_root is NOUN{
  if count(word_eco) = 1 and exists(next_word){
    if (next_word_eco contains ("ISIM_TAMLAMA_I" or "ISIM_BELIRTME"
   or "ISIM_CIKMA_DEN" or "ISIM_SAHIPLIK_SEN_IN" or
    "ISIM_TAMLAMA_IN"))
     or (next_word_root is VERB and next_word_eco contains
    ("FIIL_DONUSUM_ME" or "FIIL_EDILGENSESLI_N" or
    "FIIL_DONUSUM_IM"))
    or (next_word_root is NOUN and word is Lean and next_word is Lean)
       isPhrased=true;
   }
   else if (word_eco contains("ISIM_BULUNMA_LI" or
   "ISIM_YOKLUK_SIZ")){
     if(phrasedList.add(word_root,next_word_root); continue next;
   }
   else if (word_eco contains("ISIM_KALMA_DE") and exists(before_word)){
     if(before_word_root is VERB and !(before_word_eco
     contains("ZAMAN")))
       isPhrased=true;
   }
 }//end if word_root is NOUN
 else if (word_root is VERB){
   if (word_eco.size = 1 and next_word  is not ADJECTIVE) isPhrased=true;
   else if (word_eco contains("OLUMSUZLUK_ME") and word_eco.size = 2){
     if(next_word_root is NOUN and next_word_eco
     contains("ISIM_TAMLAMA_I")) isPhrased=true;
   }
   else if (word_eco contains("FIIL_SUREKLILIK_EREK") and
   word_eco.size = 2){
     if(exists(before_word) and before_word is NOUN)
     {    phrasedList.add(before_word_root,word_root); continue next;}
   }
   else if (word_eco contains("FIIL_BELIRTME_DIK" or
   "FIIL_DONUSUM_EN" or "FIIL_DONUSUM_IM") and
    word_eco.size >= 2){
       if (next_word_root is NOUN and next_word_eco
        contains("ISIM_TAMLAMA_DE" or "ISIM_TAMLAMA_IN" or
        "ISIM_TAMLAMA_I")) isPhrased=true;
   }
 }//end if word_root is VERB
 if (isPhrased)phrasedList.add(word_root,next_word_root);
} end for

List newPhrasedList = new List;
for each phrased_word in setBirlesikKelime{
 boolean isAdd = true;
 if((phrased_word[0] is FOREIGN_WORD) or phrased_word.size = 1 and
  phrased_word[0] is NOUN and phrased_word[0] is Lean or
  phrased_word.size = 1 and phrased_word[0].eco
  contains("ISIM_TAMLAMA_IN") or phrased_word.size = 2 and
 phrased_word[1].eco contains("ISIM_TAMLAMA_IN" or
 "ISIM_TAMLAMA_I")){
   if (exists next_phrased_word){
     if(next_phrased_word.size =1 and next_phrased_word[0].eco
      contains("ISIM_TAMLAMA_I") or next_phrased_word.size =2 and
     next_phrased_word[1].eco contains("ISIM_TAMLAMA_I")){
       List<WordSet> kList = new ArrayList(phrased_word[0]);
       if (phrased_word.size = 2) kList.add(phrased_word[1]);
       kList.add(next_phrased_word[0]);
       if (next_phrased_word.size = 2) kList.add(next_phrased_word[1]);
       newPhrasedList.add(kList);
       isAdd = false;
     }
   }
 }
 if (isAdd) { newPhrasedList.add(phrased_word);  }
}
return newPhrasedList;
```

Figure 3. Turkish Compound Word Detection Algorithm

- If it is compound and the second word has got –ın –ın suffixes.

The algorithm finally extracts the combined word list in the sentence.

This algorithm was developed to extract Turkish conjugated words and does not contain all grammar rules. To be able to contain all the rules of the Turkish language, it needs to be developed further. Since the algorithm is used on the sentences established in the daily speech language, it has been seen that not all grammatical rules are sufficient for this process in such studies. Some exclusion rules have been added to control situations such as foreign word usage.

b) Detection of Foreign Words and Abbreviations

Foreign words and abbreviations appeared as another issue to work on at tagging. Since the words in the sentence which are commonly used or which originated from traditional words used for technologies and product features cannot be solved with a Turkish natural language processor, a controlled dictionary containing these words has been created.

For these cases, the words / word groups encountered in the sentences are labeled using the abbreviations and foreign word controlled-dictionary created for these situations. Since the foreign words have been overused in the domains of the comment texts we have worked on, this controlled dictionary has produced very effective results in extracting the product features. Since the foreign words have been overused in the domains of the comment texts we have worked on, this controlled dictionary has produced very effective results in extracting the product features.

3) Detection of Frequently Repeated Product Feature

After tagging studies, an a priori algorithm was used to calculate repetition frequencies of words and word groups [16]. Repetition frequency of tagged items consisting of word roots in reviews, and the details about in which review and which sentence they appear, was kept in a file based storage environment for analysis. The reviews generally include sentences within the scope of the same topic. When opinions on the same product are combined in this way, noun and noun groups in sentences indicate product features. Frequently used words and word groups are assumed to be product features.

4) Extraction of Opinion Expressing Words

We have handled adjective and adjective expressing words in sentences to extract sentiment expressing words. Sentimental words express personal thoughts of reviewers about products. In case of multiple features in a sentence, the sentimental adjectives are evaluated relative to the most frequently repeated word or word group. Positive or negative expression forms in the Turkish language are not limited to adjectives. In order not to miss adjectives from words with the same letter clusters but different structures, adjective building statuses of suffixes rather than word stems are handled.

When we look to the stem of the word "etkileyici" in the sentence given in III.C as an example, the word "etki" does not express the meaning of an adjective. However, while the suffix "le" gives a verb meaning, the suffix "ici" makes the word an adjective and indicates a sentiment. In the method we propose, accepting the word groups that express such opinions as adjectives, sentiment sentences are revealed.

5) Extraction of Opinion Sentence Tendency

Studies on sentiment analysis aim at classification of the given text as positive, negative, or neutral. For example, it is possible that all of the reviews/comments about a soccer team or a TV program on social media are classified as positive or negative using natural language processing and text mining techniques. Here, the right situation or the wrong idea is not sought and the current situation is detected. Various methods for opinion mining may be developed. For example, distinguishing words as positive/negative and classification of reviews as positive/negative according to the number of words is one of the essential methods.

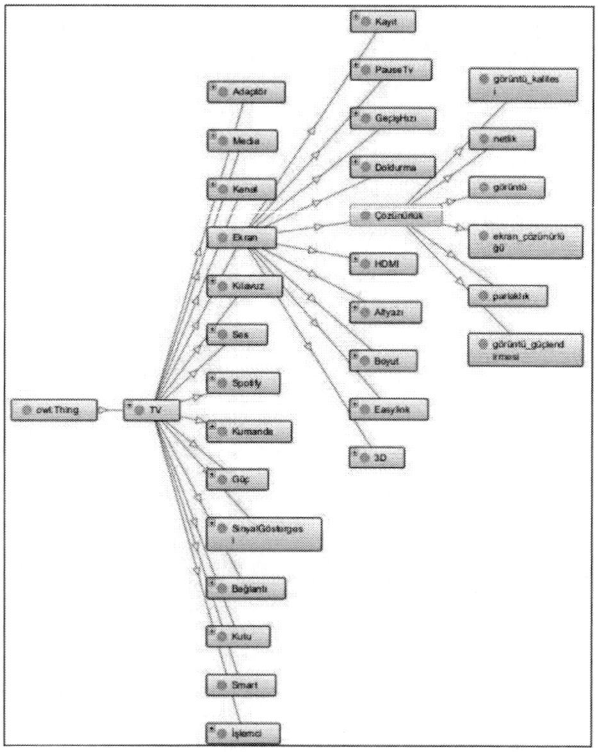

Figure 4. Ontology Diagram for Product Features – TV

While performing object-oriented opinion extraction through reviews, opinion mining through number of words, frequencies of words such as nouns, adjectives, adverbs, or verbs was a technique that we have used. In this approach, primarily noun word groups are detected, and by adding adjective word groups defining these noun word groups the infrequently repeating sentiments are eliminated. Scoring is done through adjective or adjective groups. Utilizing the adjective dictionary that exists at our disposal, the adjectives in the sentence are found to have negative or positive levels. The adjectives are subjected to these levels of aggregation and a score is calculated for the generic. All scores in the comment are summed up and a score is calculated for the comment. According to the calculation made, it is concluded that the score is positive if it is +, negative if it is - or neutral if it is 0. In this calculation, the WordOrientation and SentenceOrietation algorithms shown in the study of Hu and Liu [1] are used. The calculated scores for some features are shown in Figure 8 and Figure 13 by the OrientationScore tag.

6) Combination of Associated Words

In the processes up to this point, the identification of words which frequently repeat and express positive / negative opinions has been emphasized. Because of

```
Procedure SynonymController()
begin
for each word sentence si
begin
    var synword = synonymList.find(word.stemmed)
    if synword is not null
        word.synonymId=synword
        word.text=synword.Text
endfor;
end
```

Figure 5. Algorithm for Turkish Associated Word Extraction

variety in the grammar of the Turkish language, and the use of foreign words, we have seen that words expressing the same features have qualified as different features, and some very frequently expressed features remained under a threshold value and were not qualified as features. In order to reduce this situation as much as possible, we have focused on the integration of the words which are synonymous and express the same situation.

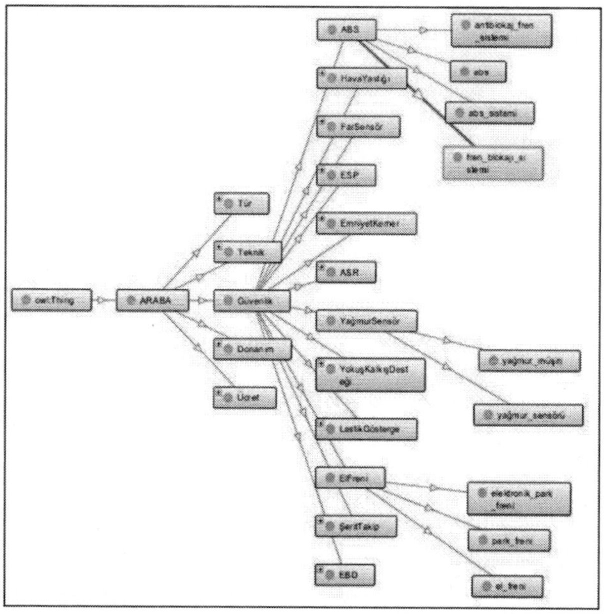

Figure 6. Ontology Diagram for Product Features - Car

Since it is not enough to check the comments one by one and remove synonyms, the abbreviations and foreign words are also grouped. For this purpose, ontologies have been created that cover the product features related to the products. These ontologies are given in Figure 4 and Figure 6.

In this way, controlled dictionaries created by experts for product specifications are created. This allows us to further increase the success of our feature extraction method. The algorithm we use is presented in Figure 5. Synonyms are detected on line 5 and values are assigned to synonyms on lines 7-8.

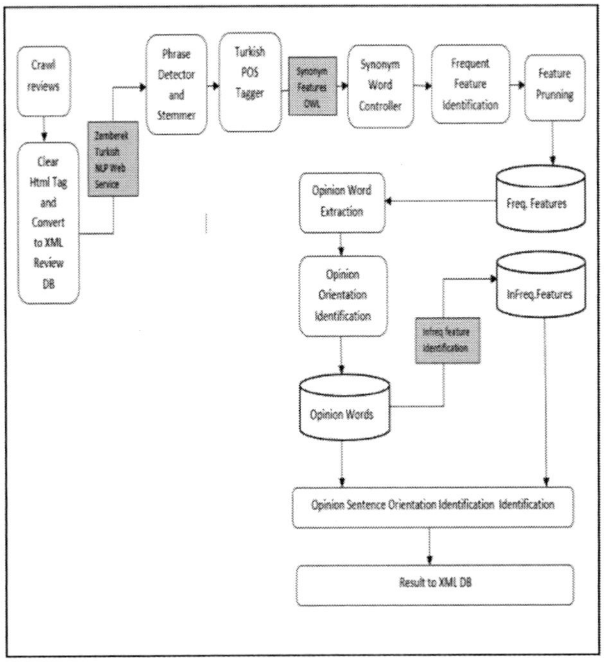

Figure 8. System Architecture Model

The flow architecture of the system is shown in Figure 7 above.

IV. IMPLEMENTATION AND EVALUATION

Our proposed methodology was implemented using C# and Java technologies. Java version 1.8.91 and C# version 4.6.1 were selected. The open source Zemberek Natural Language Processor was used as a Turkish word processor [15]; Protege 5.0.1 (protege.stanford.edu) was used for ontology development; the Jena library (jena.apache.org) has been used to process ontology data. These projects, which we use to improve our methodology, have been chosen because they are open source projects with specific developer support. The general architecture of our developed prototype software is shown in Figure 7.

The developed prototype software was designed in order to parse the product reviews performed instantly or asynchronously on the e-commerce website or product review website, to detect product features, and to perform extractions from product reviews.

In our proposed system, each idea/opinion/comment is considered to be a resource. In this structure, customers create their own comments and evaluations on e-commerce or evaluation sites.

```
<ReviewXmlDataContract>
  <ReviewID>3</ReviewID>
  <Date>2016-11-24T00:00:00</Date>
  <Author>ufuk tıkız</Author>
  <Sentences>
    <ReviewSentence>
      <SentenceId>4</SentenceId>
      <Text>ekran gayet uygun boyutlarda</Text>
      <Words>
        <ReviewWord>
          <WordId>1</WordId>
          <Tag>NOUN</Tag>
          <Text>ekran</Text>
          <StemmedText>ekran</StemmedText>
        </ReviewWord>
        <ReviewWord>
          <WordId>2</WordId>
          <Tag>ADJECTIVE</Tag>
          <Text>gayet</Text>
          <StemmedText>gayet</StemmedText>
        </ReviewWord>
        <ReviewWord>
          <WordId>3</WordId>
          <Tag>ADJECTIVE</Tag>
          <Text>uygun</Text>
          <StemmedText>uygun</StemmedText>
        </ReviewWord>
        <ReviewWord>
          <WordId>4</WordId>
          <Tag>NOUN</Tag>
          <Text>boyutlarda</Text>
          <StemmedText>boyut</StemmedText>
        </ReviewWord>
      </Words>
      <OrientationScore>3</OrientationScore>
    </ReviewSentence>
  </Sentences>
</ReviewXmlDataContract>
```

Figure 7. Parsed Review Content

Figure 8 contains this sentence as an example “ekran gayet uygun boyutlarda (the screen is of a very good size)”. Figure 8 depicts our data model of a TV model, based on the comment text entered by a user, in XML format. As can be seen from Figure 8, the data structure has upper data fields related to comment text such as Reviewld, Date, and Author. In addition, it shows the content of the text, such as "Sentenceld", "Wordld", "Text", "Tag", "StemmedText", "FrequencyId", "Synonymld", "Date", "Author" There are data items in the text that indicate the frequency of their passage in the text.

We have carried out our experiments on texts that express comments/opinions/thoughts for two different product types: Automobile and Television. We used data sets consisting of customer reviews of 5 car brands and 5 television models. Review texts were collected via "arabainceleme.com" and "hepsiburada.com" sites. For each comment text, the title of the text, the content of the text, the date and time the text was entered, the name of the author, the location of the author, and the rating value of the author are exhibited.

For each product, 100 comments were captured and downloaded by scanning the text and converted to XML documents as the example in Figure 8 shows. The texts were separated using the Zemberek Natural Language Processing library, and the words and phrases in the texts were tagged.

For each sentence in the product interpretation, these terms are tagged if they contain the user's opinions. The features of these sentences are also determined. For feature identification, the method of feature identification proposed by Hu and Liu [1] is expanded. Here, unlike the work of Hu and Liu, the synonyms and feature words are united. It also provides the tagging of the different words that have the same meaning. The terms entered for the product features entered by the users are compared with the terms of the ontologies we create to ensure that the correct product attributes are tagged. For each product, a list of features included in the comment text is produced.

TABLE I. PRODUCT FEATURES PRECISION AND RECALL RESULTS

Product Feature Extraction	Hu and Liu Approach			Proposed Approach		
Product	*Precision*	*Recall*	*F-Score*	*Precision*	*Recall*	*F-Score*
VW Golf	0.8667	0.1585	0.2680	0.9444	0.4146	0.5763
Seat Leon	0.9474	0.2195	0.3564	0.9706	0.4024	0.5690
Renault Megane	0.7667	0.5610	0.6479	0.8133	0.7439	0.7771
Opel Mokka	0.8082	0.7195	0.7613	0.8108	0.7317	0.7692
Nissan Qashqai	0.8036	0.5488	0.6522	0.8406	0.7073	0.7682
LG 32LF580N	0.6667	0.1167	0.1986	0.6885	0.9767	0.8077
Vestel 40FA5050	0.7143	0.2326	0.3509	0.8571	0.5581	0.6761
Vestel 40FB7100	0.6667	0.0667	0.1212	0.6531	0.7442	0.6957
Vestel 48FA8200	0.6429	0.2093	0.3158	0.7727	0.3953	0.5231
Vestel 48UA9300	0.7500	0.2791	0.4068	0.8667	0.6047	0.7123

For each product, the number of features extracted using the proposed method is summarized in Table 1. Here, all features in the comment text are manually tagged to determine whether the features detected by the method are correct features. Values for the recall and precision metrics were determined by comparing the properties found by our method with the properties of the products manually identified. Here, the detection of product properties (Hu and Liu's method) based on only the frequency values was compared to the frequency-based product feature detection (recommended method) attachment and discovery metrics after combining the synonymous features under a single feature. In extracting the feature count, the threshold value we use for the frequency rate is taken as 10%.

When we examine the comparison given in Table 1, we see the effect of combining the synonyms as the reason for the differences in the results. The results show that we can achieve higher finding and fixation values because of a large number of frequently used features and the presence of different feature names that mean the same. We also did the evaluation based on our product. The results are shown in

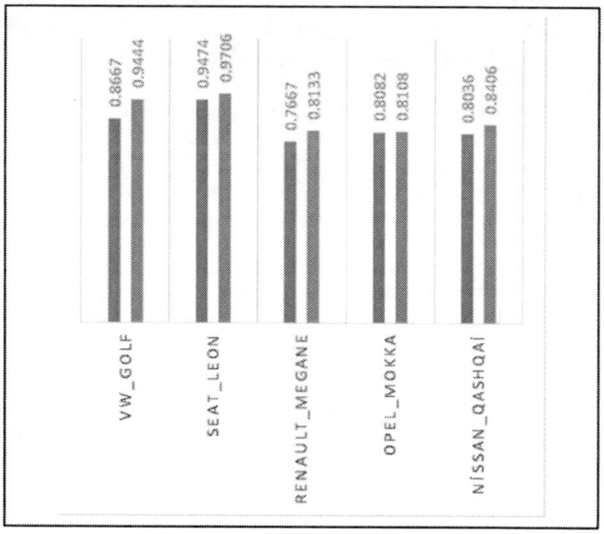

Figure 9. Precision metric values in different product feature detection approaches for automotive products

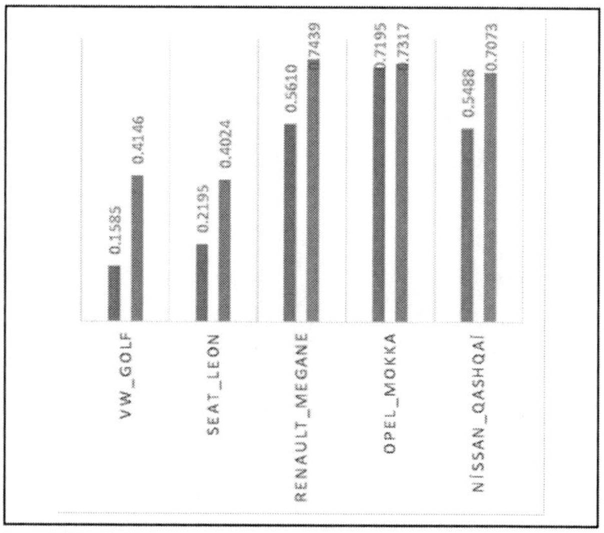

Figure 10. Recall metric values for different product feature detection approaches for automotive products

Figures 9-12. Based on the product-based evaluation, our approach suggests that it allows for more accurate traits. However, we see that the features that rarely appear in comment texts are features that are not of great interest to the general public.

Outputs from the sentiment analysis are shown in Figure 14 and Figure 15. Sentimental analysis values of the sentences we operate are calculated by taking advantage of the grades of the adjectives they possess. In this research, adjectives we have identified in the sentence are assigned values from a controlled list composed of rated adjective words and word groups. The values corresponding to the adjectives that existed in the properties we extracted were given value assignments at the frequency of repetition of the properties and sentiment analysis values were obtained. Each of the rated adjectives in our hand is rated as positive (1), negative (-1), or neutral (0). These sentimental analysis values given to the extracted features are calculated in proportion to the frequency of repetition of the feature, the frequency of the adjectives it possesses, and the grades of these adjectives.

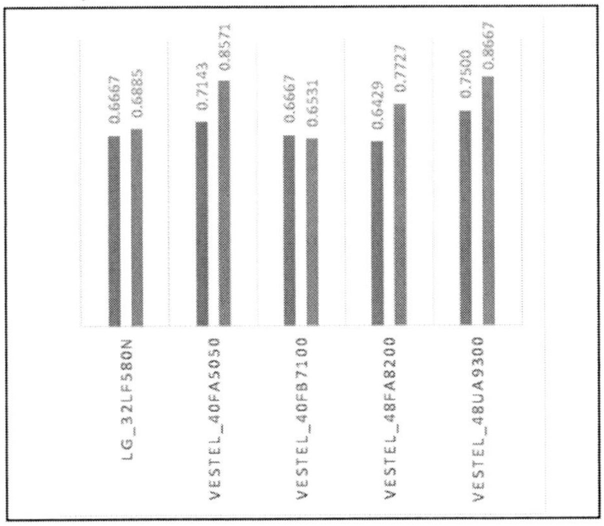

Figure 11. Precision metric values for different product feature detection approaches for TV model

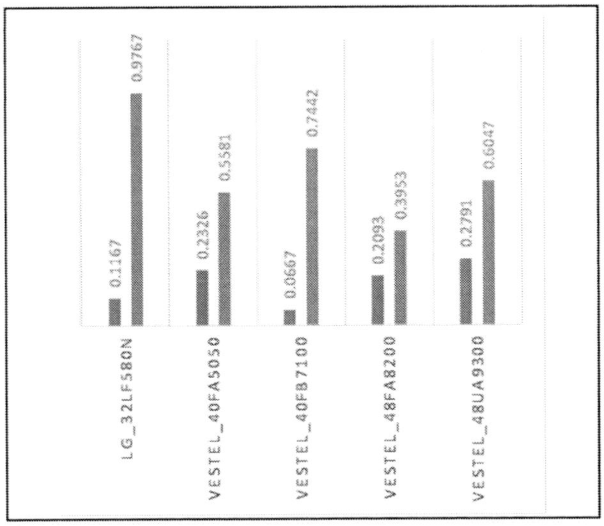

Figure 12. Recall metric values for different product feature detection approaches for TV model

Figure 13 deals with the statement "Ancak(CON) donanım (NOUN) konusunda (NOUN) eksik (ADJ)", (however, the hardware is a bit lacking). The approach we have proposed is that the "donanım konusu" sentence is a compound word. "eksik" is perceived as a negative adjective.

```
<ReviewSentence
xsi:type="ReviewSentenceWithOrientation">
  <SentenceId>7</SentenceId>
  <Text>Ancak donanım konusunda eksik.</Text>
  <Words>
    <ReviewWord>
      <WordId>1</WordId>
      <Tag>CONNECTIVE</Tag>
      <Text>ancak</Text>
      <StemmedText>ancak</StemmedText>
    </ReviewWord>
    <ReviewWord xsi:type="ReviewPhraseWord">
      <WordId>2</WordId>
      <Tag>NOUN</Tag>
      <Text>donanım konusunda</Text>
      <StemmedText>donanım konu</StemmedText>
    </ReviewWord>
    <ReviewWord>
      <WordId>3</WordId>
      <Tag>ADJECTIVE</Tag>
      <Text>eksik</Text>
      <StemmedText>eksik</StemmedText>
    </ReviewWord>
  </Words>
  <OrientationScore>-1</OrientationScore>
</ReviewSentence>
```

Figure 13. Sentence Example for Output of Sentiment Analysis

When viewed in this way, the word "donanım konusu" is marked as a property by being associated with the "donanım" attribute from the ontology diagram, and has a score of -1 in the sentiment analysis calculation because it is passed along with a negative adjective.

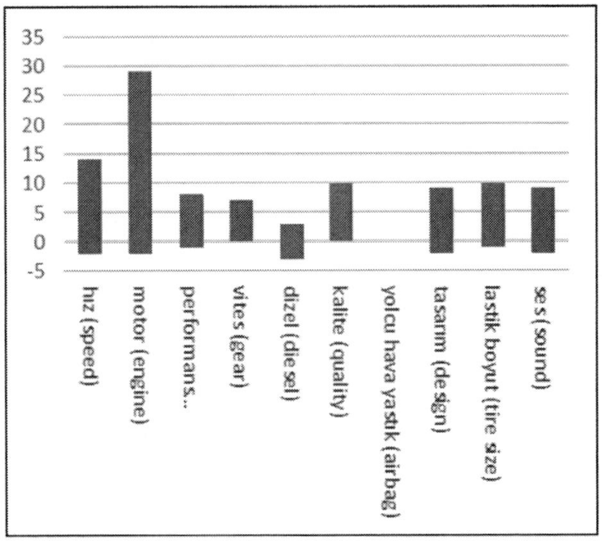

Figure 14. Sentiment Analysis values for the top 10 features in the VW Golf car

The sentiment analysis results of the features that we have obtained and shown with OrientationScore tag, appear in Figure 14 and Figure 15. While positive comments gain weight in some features, some seem to gain negative comments, others are neutral. These figures give us information about the good and bad features of the products.

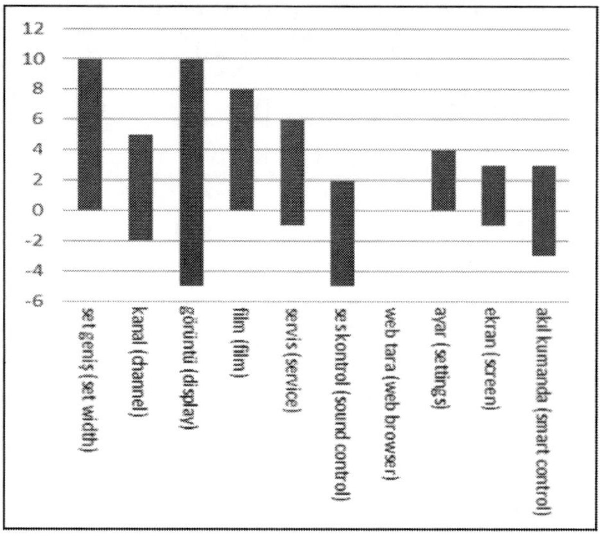

Figure 15. Sentiment Analysis values for the top 10 features of Vestel 48FA200 television

V. RESULTS AND FUTURE WORK

Within the scope of this research, a method is proposed that can process the Turkish comments made by customers for the products sold online, automatically extract the features of the products, and then summarize the positive or negative opinions of the customers based on the product features.

The methodology we propose and the software we have developed for this methodology yields very successful results in deriving the actual features used in the sentence. The experiments we have conducted to test the success of our proposed method have shown the effectiveness of our proposed approach, including the fact that the recall and precision metric values we obtained in the results are high.

Within the scope of this study, the performance ratios for product feature inferences were tested from texts that expressed comments / opinions / ideas. In future studies, we will develop our ontologies to extract product features more effectively. In addition to this, we will expand the scope of our experiments by increasing the number of texts that specify the comments / opinions / thoughts we have selected.

ACKNOWLEDGMENT

This study is being supported by the TUBITAK-3501-Career Development Program (CAREER) with the Project ID: 114E781.

REFERENCES

[1] M. Hu and B. Liu. "Mining and summarizing customer reviews". *In Proceedings of ACM-KDD 2004*, pp.168-177.

[2] R. Kumar V. and K. Raghuveer. "Web User Opinion Analysis for Product Features Extraction and Opinion Summarization". *International Journal of Web & Semantic Technology (IJWesT) Vol.3, No.4, October 2012*, pp.69.

[3] V. Brindha and M. Kathiravan "Text Mining For Infrequent Noun Feature Extraction And Sentiment Classification". *International Journal of Emerging Technology in Computer Science & Electronics (IJETCSE), ISSN: 0976-1353 Volume 13 Issue 4 – March 2015*, pp.323-326.

[4] S. H. Ghorashi, R. Ibrahim, S. Noekhah, and N. S. Dastjerdi "A Frequent Pattern Mining Algorithm for Feature Extraction of Customer Reviews". *IJCSI International Journal of Computer Science Issues, Vol. 9, Issue 4, No 1, July 2012*, pp.29-35.

[5] L. Ferreira, N. Jakob, and I. Gurevych "A Comparative Study of Feature Extraction Algorithms in Customer Reviews". *2008 IEEE International Conference on Semantic Computing, August 2008*, pp.144-151.

[6] L. Zhuang, F. Jing, and X. Zhu "Movie review mining and summarization", *Proceedings of the 15th ACM international conference on Information and knowledge management, Virginia, November 2006*, pp.43-50.

[7] Harvard Business Review Analytic Services Report, *Marketing in the driver's seat: Using Analytics to create customer value February 2016*

[8] P. D. Turney, "Thumbs Up or Thumbs Down Semantic Orientation Applied to Unsupervised Classification of Reviews". *Proceedings of the 40th Annual Meeting on Association for Computational Linguistics, July 2002, Philadelphia*, pp.417-424.

[9] B. Pang, L. Lee, and S. Vaithyanathan "Thumbs up? Sentiment Classification Using Machine Learning Techniques." *Procedings of the Conference on Empirical Methods in Natural Language Processing (EMNLP), Philadelphia, July 2002*, pp.78-96.

[10] I. Mani and E. Bloedorn "Multi-document Summarization by Graph Search and Matching". *Procedings of the 14th national conference on artificial intelligence and 9th conference on Innovative applications of artificial intelligence, Rhode Island, July 1997*, pp.622-628.

[11] J. Yi and W. Niblack "Sentiment Mining in WebFountain". *Proceedings of the 21st International Conference on Data Engineering, April 2005, Volume 0*, pp.1073-1083.

[12] V. Hatzivassiloglou and J. Wiebe "Effects of Adjective Orientation and Gradability on Sentence Subjectivity". *Proceedings of the 18th conference on Computational linguistics - Volume 1*, pp.299-305.

[13] M. Hearst "Direction-based Text Interpretation as an Information Access Refinement". *In Paul Jacobs, editor, Text-Based Intelligent Systems. Lawrence Erlbaum Associates, 1992*, pp.257-274..

[14] R. Tong "An Operational System for Detecting and Tracking Opinions in on-line discussion" *SIGIR 2001 Workshop on Operational Text Classification, Volume 1*, p 6.

[15] A.A. Akın and M.D. Akın "Zemberek, an open source NLP framework for Turkic Languages" https://github.com/ahmetaa/zemberek-nlp [retrieved: 04, 2017]

[16] F. Coenen "LUCS KDD implementation of CBA", Department of Computer Science, The University of Liverpool http://www.csc.liv.ac.uk/~frans/KDD/Software/CMAR/cba.html [retrieved: 04, 2017]

Decentralized Bootstrapping for WebRTC-based P2P Networks

Dennis Boldt, Felix Kaminski and Stefan Fischer
Institute of Telematics
University of Lübeck
Lübeck, Germany
Email: {boldt,kaminski,fischer}@itm.uni-luebeck.de

***Abstract*—Around the millennium, peer-to-peer (P2P) networks were standalone applications, where users had to configure their firewalls properly to be able to connect to the network. Nowadays, P2P connections between browsers are possible without the need for any user-side configuration. This can be achieved with the Web Real-Time Communication protocol stack (WebRTC). Recent research showed that WebRTC-based peer-to-peer networks can work as a decentralized, redundant and encrypted storage for user data. However, all existing networks employ a centralized bootstrapping infrastructure, which still is a single point of failure. In this paper, we present a decentralized architecture to handle bootstrapping for a WebRTC-based peer-to-peer network, completely removing the need for a central instance. The architecture uses the highly decentralized Domain Name System (DNS), combined with so-called Master-Peers. Our evaluation shows that the architecture scales well and reduces the bootstrapping time remarkably.**

***Keywords*–Peer-to-Peer; Decentralized; Bootstrapping; WebRTC; Chord; DNS**

I. Introduction

The Internet changed in the last 20 years. In the 1990s, the Internet was a consume-only network, where content providers produced the content, and people consumed it. Starting in the 2000s, the Internet changed to a user-generated content network. Thus, new web technologies and protocols were designed to support that shift. In 2006, the first technology was the XMLHttpRequest (XHR) [1]. XHR provides asynchronous HTTP requests without page reloading. To get real-time updates from the server, a client needs to perform XHR requests frequently. In 2009, a first draft of the WebSockets Protocol was published [2]. The main benefit of the WebSockets Protocol is that connections are bidirectional. It can be used by a server to push data to a client immediately.

To enable browser-to-browser communication, Web Real-Time Communication (WebRTC) was developed in recent years [3], [4] (see Section II-C).

The main challenge of every P2P network is *bootstrapping*, which is the initial creation of the network itself and new peers joining it. This is still a challenge for classical P2P networks [5], [6], thus we review some typical bootstrapping methods in Section II-A. As bootstrapping is a core functionality inherent to P2P, it is also required for WebRTC-based P2P networks.

Our contribution in this paper is a decentralized architecture to handle bootstrapping for a WebRTC-based P2P network, which avoids having a single point of failure (SPOF). WebRTC still needs servers to exchange meta data and to cope with Network Address Translators (NATs) [7]. We achieve the bootstrapping by deploying these servers behind DNS-based load balancers around the world. These servers are used in combination with a geolocation approach.

The remainder of this paper is organized as follows: Section II gives an overview on the fundamentals. Related work on browser-based P2P networks is presented in Section III, our bootstrapping architecture is presented in Section IV, and Section V shows experimental results. Finally, the paper ends with a conclusion and future work in Section VI.

II. Fundamentals

If a component is both a consumer and a producer, it needs both client and server functionality and is then called a peer. A network which connects directly multiple peers is called a P2P network. In such a network, peers can communicate directly without the need for a central server. P2P networks are so-called *overlay networks*. They can be classified as *structured* or *unstructured* [8]. Unstructured networks establish connections between peers in an arbitrary manner, e.g., Gnutella [9] or Kazaa [10]. Here, the location of data is not known. To find data, a peer has to flood the entire network. In structured networks, peers have unique identifiers and the location of data can be associated with a specific peer, e.g., Kademlia [11] or Chord [12]. Because of this, the network behaves like a Distributed Hash Table (DHT). Structured networks organize themselves in topologies:

Full mesh: In a full mesh topology, every peer is connected to every other peer. A joining peer needs to establish a connection to every peer in the network.

Star: In a star topology, every peer is connected to a central peer. The problem of the star topology is that all messages are routed through the central peer which conforms to the classical client-server architecture.

Ring: A common P2P topology is the ring topology. The number of connections in the network depends on the ring algorithm. In Chord, every peer maintains a so-called finger table of size $log_2(N)$.

Tree: A binary tree is another common topology for P2P networks. Examples are Kademlia [11] or P-Grid [13].

A. Bootstrapping Methods

Research in the area of bootstrapping was done by GauthierDickey and Grothoff [15], Cramer et al. [5] or Knoll et al. [16]. They divide the existing bootstrapping methods into *peer-based* and *mediator-based* approaches:

1) Peer-based approaches: These approaches involve technologies where peers can find other peers without the need for a third party.

a) A *Peer Cache* is a database of peers to which a peer was connected previously. To join the network, a peer

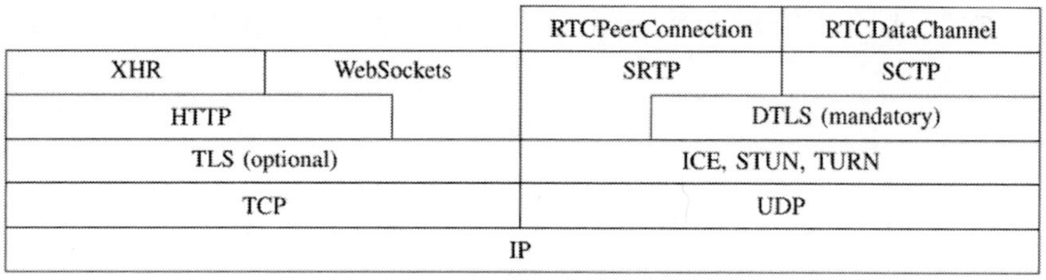

Figure 1. WebRTC protocol stack (Based on [14]).

tries to connect to one peer in its cache. If that fails, the joining peer tries the next peers from the cache. If all peers fail, or a peer joins the P2P network for the first time, a fallback is needed, e.g., a rendezvous server (see below).

b) *Multicast/Broadcast*: Peers in a Local Area Network (LAN) join a multicast group. A joining peer sends a request to that group. As a reply, the peer receives some peers to which it can connect. This approach works well for Universal Plug and Play (UPnP) or zero-configuration networking (Zeroconf) within a LAN, but it does not scale for world-wide networks.

c) *Random IP Probing*: A joining peer randomly selects Internet Protocol (IP) addresses [17] and tries to connect to a specific port. If a host is a peer of the network already, it answers according to the bootstrapping protocol. If not, the joining peer tries another IP address. Obviously, this does not scale on the Internet.

2) Mediator-based approaches: A mediator is a so called *well-known entry point*, which must be known prior to bootstrapping. This entry point should never change and must always be available. Mediators can be peers of the network or separate hosts.

a) *Rendezvous Server*: A rendezvous server is a central server to which a joining peer can connect. The rendezvous server returns a list of active peers, or it forwards the joining request to a peer in the network. This approach is used by Napster [18] as a central index, and by BitTorrent [19], where it is called tracker.

b) *Internet Relay Chat*: Knoll et al. [16] propose to use the Internet Relay Chat (IRC) [20] for bootstrapping, because it is a highly decentralized architecture. A joining peer connects to an IRC channel, where it can communicate with all peers. IRC is a widely distributed and failure tolerant decentralized network, thus it is quite reliable.

B. Bootstrapping Requirements

Bootstrapping can be organized centralized or decentralized. If bootstrapping is centralized, it uses a single central bootstrapping server following the client-server approach, which is a SPOF. The opposite is decentralized bootstrapping, where all components of the bootstrapping are decentralized. Knoll et al. [16] propose five requirements for a decentralized bootstrapping architecture:

1) Robustness against Failure: All components of the bootstrapping should be completely decentralized and the bootstrapping should not exhibit a SPOF, e.g., no central bootstrapping server.

2) Robustness against Security Appliances: Users should not have trouble with their NATs, e.g., users cannot connect to the P2P network without configuring port forwarding.

3) Robustness against External Inference: All components of the bootstrapping should be decentralized. No entity is able to shut down elemental components of the bootstrapping. Additionally, the bootstrapping should still work if the initiator leaves, thus other peers take over the tasks of the initiator.

4) Efficiency: The bootstrapping should be fast and lightweight. This could be the number of messages exchanged for bootstrapping or joining of a peer should happen in a reasonable amount of time.

5) Scalability: The bootstrap must scale with the number of peers in the network.

C. WebRTC

Web Real-Time Communication (WebRTC) does not reinvent the wheel, it is a protocol stack (see Figure 1) based on existing protocols [3] and combines them into the corresponding WebRTC API [4]. WebRTC is used to establish direct P2P connections between two browsers, based on *RTCMediaStreams* [21] and *RTCDataChannels* [22]. Most WebRTC projects are focused on multimedia applications such as telephone conferences and use RTCMediaStreams. RTCDataChannels are a universal channel type in binary-format. They are implemented through encapsulating the Stream Control Transmission Protocol (SCTP) over the User Datagram Protocol (UDP) [23] (SCTP-over-UDP), which allows the configuration of reliability and in-order-delivery without using the Transmission Control Protocol (TCP) [24].

In order to establish a browser-to-browser P2P connection, WebRTC uses the well-known *Offer/Answer Model* [25] from the Session Initiation Protocol (SIP) [26]. This includes *offer* and *answer* messages serialized with the Session Description Protocol (SDP) [27], which contain media capabilities, e.g., for the Real-Time Transport Protocol (RTP) [28]. Additionally, WebRTC collects connectivity information with Interactive Connectivity Establishment (ICE) [29] to search for the most efficient connection between two peers. This is done in three steps: Gathering ICE candidates, exchange offer/answer messages and ICE candidates, and finally running connectivity checks.

In the first step, ICE gathers so-called *ICE candidates*, which are transport addresses (e.g., IP/port tuples) of three types:

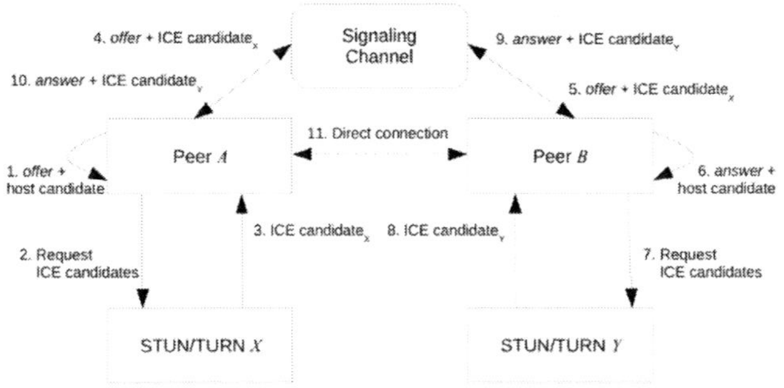

Figure 2. WebRTC Offer/Answer Model, including the offer/answer messages, ICE candidates and the signaling channel.

1) Host Candidates: They contain the local transport address and are obtained directly from the local network interface.

2) Server Reflexive Candidates: They contain the public transport address from the public side of a NAT, which is usually not known to peers behind a NAT. They are obtained by using Session Traversal Utilities for NAT (STUN) [30]. STUN connects via UDP to an external STUN-server, which returns the public transport address. STUN can also be used to keep a public transport address binding alive.

3) Relay Candidates: They contain an external transport address from a publicly available relay server. They are obtained by using Traversal Using Relays around NAT (TURN) [31], which connects to a TURN server, which itself binds a transport address and returns that to the peer.

In the second step, offer/answer messages and ICE candidates are exchanged between two peers through a so-called *Signaling Channel*, which implementation is not specified in WebRTC, so it could be XHR or WebSockets (left side of Figure 1).

Finally, the third step pairs the candidates and both peers perform connectivity checks with all ICE candidate-pairs to see, which pairs work:

1): ICE tries a direct connection with the Host Candidates, e.g., within LANs.

2): If that fails, ICE tries to connect to the Server Reflex Candidates. In case of a Full Cone NAT [32], any peer can send packets to that public transport address, which forwards them to the local transport address of the peer behind the NAT.

3): If this fails as well, i.e., a peer is behind a Symmetric NAT [32], only the initial external host (e.g., the STUN server) can send a packet back to the peer behind the NAT. The fallbacks are the Relay Candidates.

Figure 2 shows all required steps to establish a direct P2P connection with the WebRTC Offer/Answer Model: Peer A creates an offer and initiates a communication with a STUN/-TURN server, and as a result, A receives ICE candidates (steps 1 to 3). Both the offer and the ICE candidates are sent to peer B through the signaling channel (steps 4 and 5). As soon as B receives the offer, it creates an answer and performs the same process (steps 6 to 8) and sends its connectivity information through the same signaling channel back to A (steps 9 and 10). After the signaling is complete, both peers have all connectivity information: answer, offer and both ICE candidates. Finally, both peers perform connectivity-checks with all ICE candidate-pairs to establish a direct connection to each other (step 11).

Observation 1: WebRTC-based P2P networks always require two components for bootstrapping: A signaling mechanism to exchange the offer/answer messages and the ICE candidates (e.g., a signaling server), and a STUN/TURN server to establish connections from/to peers behind NATs. Consequently, WebRTC-based P2P networks are always hybrid P2P networks.

III. RELATED WORK

Vogt et al. presented BOPlish in 2013 [33], [34]. They claim that their approach is not supposed to operate on Internet-scale. They use one central bootstrap server, which holds a number of WebSocket connections to peers that have recently joined the network. Thus, a joining peer is able to perform the signaling over these WebSocket connections. If all recently joined peers have left the network, a joining peer will not be able to join the network anymore. Their future work included a JavaScript implementation of Chord.

In 2014, we presented a browser-based P2P network [35]. Our network was based on a so-called *WebSocket SOCKS5 Proxy* (WSSP). Browsers are connecting to the WSSP with WebSockets, where they use the SOCKS5 protocol, Like this, a browser is able to connect to other browsers through the WSSP. We also use the WSSP as the central bootstrapping component. because it is used to handle bootstrapping and to proxy connections. We implemented Chord in JavaScript to create a P2P ring topology. Our future work included a WebRTC-based network.

In parallel, Vogt et al. continued their work on BOPlish which was presented in 2014 [36]. Like our approach, they use Chord to create a P2P ring topology. They refer to a *bootstrapping component* which handles WebRTC specifics like offers and answers. Unfortunately, they do not explain protocol details.

Desprat et al. presented a hybrid client-server and P2P network for a collaborative Computer Aided Design (CAD) in 2015 [37]. Their approach is not designed to operate on Internet-scale. It is made for a small group of peers (max. 7-8 users). They create a WebRTC-based P2P full mesh topology between all peers. The P2P network is used to distribute real-time updates, and a client-server architecture (based on XHR) to persist the CAD data. The bootstrapping uses Peer.js [38]: A new peer connects to a central server which returns a list of Identifiers (IDs) of all existing peers in the network. Now, the new peer connects to a signaling server via WebSockets and gets an ID. The new peer can initiate the signaling and connects to all peers.

Disterhöft and Graffi proposed a WebRTC-based P2P network for social networks in 2015 [39]. Their implementation is based on the Google Web Toolkit (GWT) [40], which allows to create web applications in Java. In Java they used OpenChord [41] to create a ring topology. OpenChord uses native TCP/IP connections, thus they modified it to use Peer.js. Peer.js is used to perform the signaling and to create the connections. As before, the drawback of this approach is the central Peer.js server to handle the bootstrapping, which again is a SPOF.

Bille et al. published RTCSS in 2016 [42]. RTCSS provides an API to create objects that are synchronized between browsers, using a publish/subscribe pattern. For bootstrapping, they use a centralized socket.io-based signaling server [43]. When a new peer connects to this server, it receives its ID and a list of peer IDs existing in the network (similar to Peer.js). Then, the new peer connects to each peers using signaling. Consequently, the peers form a full mesh network. This is unsuitable for very large WebRTC-based networks, as the number of WebRTC connections per browser is limited.

Observation 2: All existing WebRTC-based P2P networks exhibit one SPOF, by using a central bootstrapping.

IV. Bootstrapping Architecture

This section presents a decentralized bootstrapping architecture for WebRTC-based P2P networks, which resolves Observation 2. We start by analyzing the bootstrapping methods from Section II-A, to figure out which methods do work in the context of WebRTC:

Using a *Peer Cache* requires peers to exchange connectivity information to reconnect to a previously known peer. A WebRTC peer has no way to initiate this exchange, once all WebRTC connections are closed. *Multicast/Broadcast* relies on packet forwarding, which is usually not enabled on Internet routers. Consequently, broadcast is not suited for WebRTC. *Random IP Probing* requires peers to listen on a specific port for incoming connections, which is not possible with WebRTC. *IRC* is a protocol built on top of TCP. Using IRC is not feasible in an WebRTC environment, since clients cannot connect directly to TCP sockets. A *Rendezvous Server* acts as a third party, which a browser can reach by using XHR or WebSockets.

As required in *Observation 1*, WebRTC needs a signaling server and a STUN/TURN server. Thus, the only possible bootstrapping method for WebRTC-based P2P networks are Rendezvous Servers. Knoll et al. [16] use the IRC for bootstrapping, because it is an existing, highly decentralized architecture. Since we cannot use IRC, our goal is to use an existing, highly decentralized architecture for bootstrapping as well: The Domain Name System (DNS) [44].

A. Slave Peers and Master Peers

We define that a peer can operate in two ways, *Master* and *Slave*:

Slave Peers are regular peers in the Chord ring. They don't have any special functionalities, except those which are needed for the Chord protocol. Thus, they are perfectly suited for browser environments.

Master Peers are regular peers and act as STUN/TURN servers and as signaling servers, with access to the Chord ring via RTCDataChannels. For STUN/TURN, they need to listen on a fixed port. Consequently, they can only run in a server environment.

B. Signaling Channel

To join the network, peer A connects via WebSockets to a Master Peer M and sends a *findSuccessor*-request, which M forwards in-network via WebRTC to the corresponding peer B. Both, the WebSocket connection between peer A and M as well as the in-network WebRTC connections are the signaling channel to be used for the Offer/Answer Model as explained in Section II-C. A *Signaling Channel* is shown in Figure 3. Having a higher Round Trip Time (RTT) between A and M results in a higher bootstrapping time.

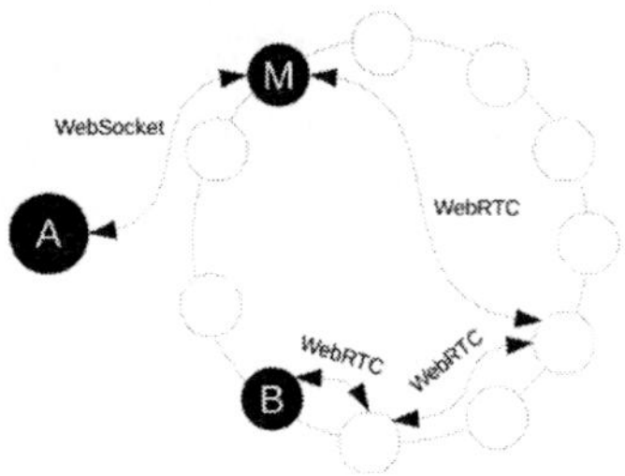

Figure 3. Signaling Channel.

Therefore, our goal is to reduce the RTT of this connection in the next subsections.

C. Scalable Bootstrapping

To allow a scalable way of managing signaling server addresses, we use a load balancer which uses DNS Round Robin Load Balancing [45]. The load balancer only serves as a public DNS entry (i.e., a domain) for some associated Master Peers (see Figure 4). Joining peers do not need to know IP addresses of any specific Master Peer, but only the domain of the load balancer. The DNS lookup returns the IP address of one associated Master Peer and a new peer can join the network.

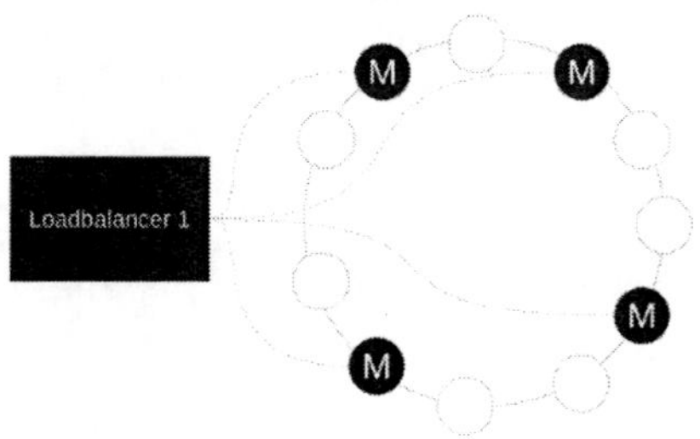

Figure 4. Scalable Bootstrapping.

D. Multiple Load Balancers

As it can be seen in Figure 4, the load balancer is now the SPOF. Therefore, we extend our architecture with multiple DNS-based load balancers, each one with a set of associated Master Peers. This can be seen in Figure 5 (other peers exists between the Master Peers, but are not shown). The Master Peers are located geographically close to the load balancers. Thus, the RTT to the Master Peers is similar to the RTT to the load balancer.

E. Geolocated Bootstrapping

To reduce bootstrapping times, we also use a geolocation-based approach with a distributed set of load balancers around the world. The associated Master Peers are still geographically

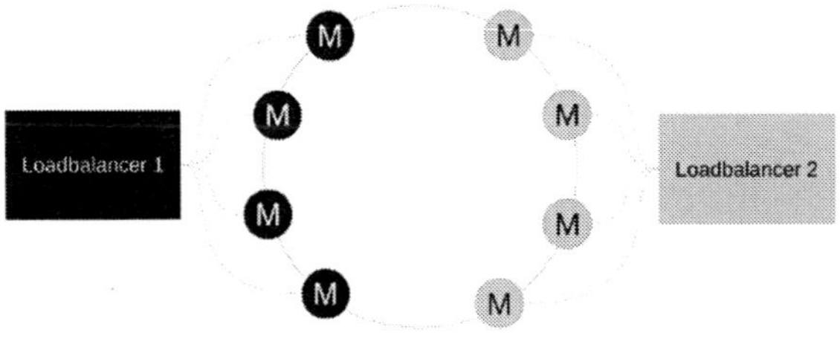

Figure 5. Multiple Load Balancers.

close to the load balancers. The P2P application itself is distributed with a load balancer list with their corresponding latitude- and longitude-coordinates. Given two load balancers and a peer A wants to join the network. It uses the native Geolocation API to retrieve its approximate latitude- and longitude-coordinates. By knowing the coordinates of the load balancers, A connects to the closest available load balancer.

The geolocated bootstrapping only reduces the WebSocket RTT and the STUN/TURN RTT to the Master Peer of the bootstrapping process. Given a global Chord ring, one cannot guarantee that a peer connects to a successor close to it, e.g., the same country or the same continent.

V. Evaluation

A. Experimental Setup and Results

To evaluate our architecture, we use *Amazon Web Services – Elastic Compute Cloud* (AWS EC2) instances and AWS Elastic Load Balancers, which use DNS Round Robin Load Balancing. Each Master Peer can be started through Amazon Machine Images (AMIs) and can be automatically registered to the load balancer in an AWS Auto Scaling Group. As a STUN/TURN server, we use coTURN [46]. We only measure the bootstrapping time from a joining peer A in central Europe (located in Lübeck) to one Master Peer M, deployed in each AWS region. Like this, we prevent in-network messages, which can span the whole globe. We divide the measurement into three steps:

1) TCP and WebSocket handshake time,
2) Chord time, e.g., from *findSuccessor*-Request until the successor is returned, and
3) WebRTC process time, until the connection is opened (incl. offer, answer, ICE).

Figure 6 shows our result, which is an average value for 25 tests per region. It can be seen, that the bootstrapping increases with the distance to the Master Peer. Bootstrapping with a Master Peer in region *eu-central-1* (Frankfurt) needs 778ms, while bootstrapping with a Master Peer in region *ap-southeast-2* (Sydney) needs 3777ms. This shows, that our decentralized bootstrapping reduces the bootstrapping time remarkably. The box plots in Figure 7 show the detailed distribution of the three evaluated steps.

26 messages are exchanged between a joining peer A and a Master Peer M during the bootstrapping process:

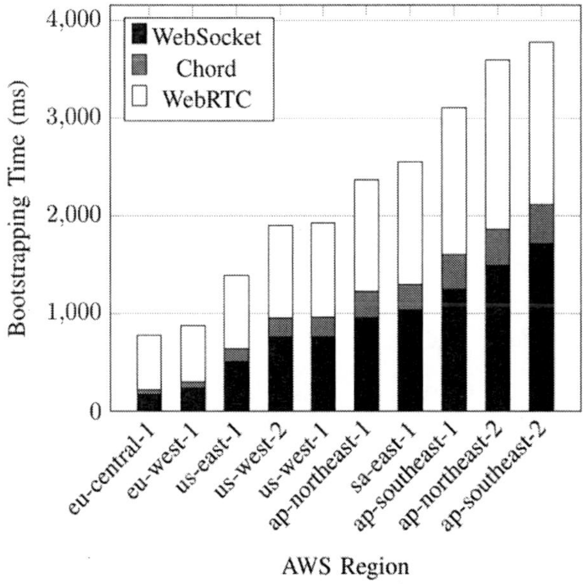

Figure 6. Average value for 25 tests per AWS region.

TCP and WebSocket handshake (4 messages)
A sends a TCP-SYN to M receives a TCP-ACK from M
A sends WebSocket-request to M and receives the response

Chord (2 messages)
A sends the findSuccessor-request to M and receives the findSuccessor-response

WebRTC (20 messages)
A sends a STUN request to M and receives a Server Reflexive Candidate
A sends a TURN request to M and receives a Relay Candidate
A sends the offer to M and receives an acknowledgement
A sends the Host Candidate to M and receives an acknowledgement
A sends the Server Reflexive Candidate to M and receives an acknowledgement
A sends the Server Relay Candidate M and receives an acknowledgement
A receives the answer from M and sends an acknowledgement
A receives the Host Candidate to M and sends an acknowledgement
A receives the Server Reflexive Candidate to M and sends an acknowledgement
A receives the Server Relay Candidate M and sends an acknowledgement

This number of messages is the smallest possible with WebRTC.

B. Bootstrapping Requirements

Finally we evaluate our bootstrapping wrt. to Section II-B:

1) Robustness against Failure: We have a geolocated bootstrapping with multiple load balancers and multiple Master Peers. Thus, we do not have a SPOF.

2) Robustness against Security Appliances: WebRTC uses STUN/TURN and ICE, which handles peers behind NATs. Therefore, user do not have to configure any port forwarding.

3) Robustness against External Inference: All components of the bootstrapping are decentralized. Even if the initial Master Peer leaves the Auto Scaling Group, other Master Peers will be available.

4) Efficiency: Because of the geolocated bootstrapping, a peer always selects the closest load balancer. The RTT to a Master Peer is small and the bootstrapping happens in the shortest possible time (see Section V-A). The number of messages exchanged is the smallest possible with WebRTC.

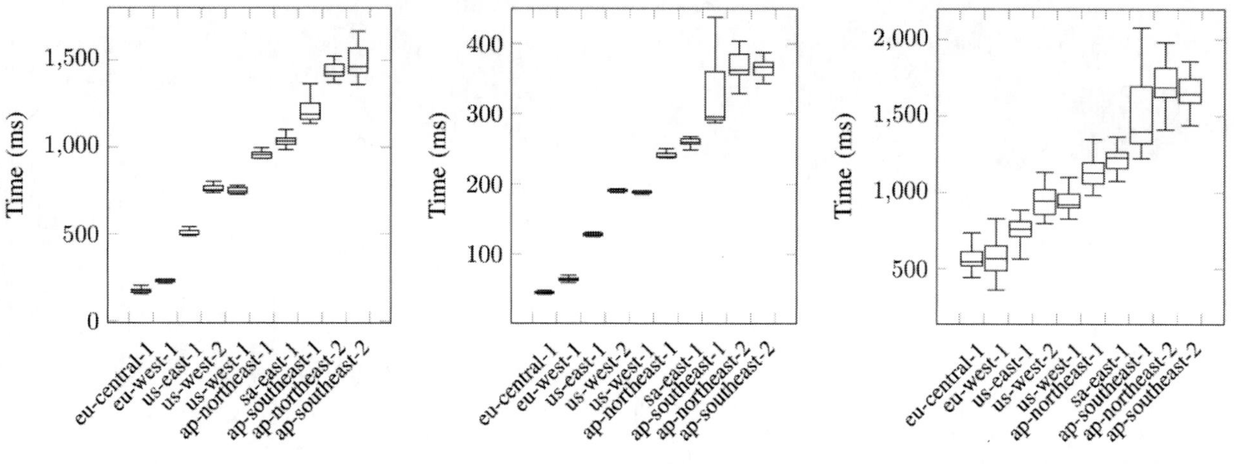

(a) TCP and WebSocket handshake time.

(b) Chord time.

(c) WebRTC process time.

Figure 7. Detailed distribution of the three evaluation steps.

5) Scalability: If the load gets high, additional Master Peers associated with the load balancer will be started automatically by the Auto Scaling Group. If the load gets low, Master Peers are removed. Thus, our bootstrapping scales. Additionally, the DNS is a well-working decentralized and scalable system, thus we rely on it.

All requirements are covered. So, we achieved a decentralized bootstrapping architecture for a WebRTC-based P2P network. Note that just the bootstrapping is decentralized. WebRTC-based P2P networks itself are still hybrid P2P networks, because they require a signaling server and a STUN/-TURN server. These servers are addressed with well-known domains.

VI. Conclusion and Future work

In this paper, we described a decentralized architecture to handle the bootstrapping for WebRTC-based P2P networks. Our architecture is based on Master Peers associated with a DNS-based load balancer. We have chosen DNS, because it is an existing, highly decentralized architecture which is used by browsers. Additionally, we employed a geolocation-based bootstrapping to reduce the bootstrapping time.

Our future work is mainly focused on security. Feher et al. [47] provide an overview on the security of WebRTC, which can be a starting point in order to improve our bootstrapping architecture. Since we use the DNS Round Robin Load Balancing for bootstrapping, Domain Name System Security Extensions (DNSSEC) [48] must be taken into account. Because STUN and TURN support TLS-over-TCP, a secure connection to the STUN/TURN server can be used by ICE to collect the connectivity information. WebSockets support TLS-over-TCP as well, thus the connection to the Master Peer can be secured too. For TLS it is possible to use certificates issued by Let's Encrypt [49], since they support the Automatic Certificate Management Environment (ACME) protocol [50]. The established WebRTC connections between the peers are secured per specification of the WebRTC protocol. Even all connections are secured, intermediate nodes in the P2P network are still able to eavesdrop and to modify the bootstrapping messages (i.e., connectivity information, offer and answer messages). Thus, a confidential and authenticated end-to-end connection to exchange the bootstrapping messages is required.

References

[1] A. van Kesteren, J. Aubourg, J. Song, and H. Steen, "XMLHttpRequest Level 2," W3C Working Group Note, Nov. 2014. [Online]. Available: http://www.w3.org/TR/XMLHttpRequest2/ [retrieved: April, 2017]

[2] I. Fette and A. Melnikov, "The WebSocket Protocol," RFC 6455 (Proposed Standard), Internet Engineering Task Force, Dec. 2011. [Online]. Available: http://www.ietf.org/rfc/rfc6455.txt [retrieved: April, 2017]

[3] H. Alvestrand, "Overview: Real time protocols for browser-based applications," Internet Engineering Task Force, Internet Draft, draft-ietf-rtcweb-overview-18, Mar. 2017. [Online]. Available: https://tools.ietf.org/html/draft-ietf-rtcweb-overview-18 [retrieved: April, 2017]

[4] A. Bergkvist, D. C. Burnett, C. Jennings, A. Narayanan, and B. Aboba, "WebRTC 1.0: Real-time communication between browsers," World Wide Web Consortium, Working Draft, WD-webrtc-20170313, Mar. 2017. [Online]. Available: https://www.w3.org/TR/2017/WD-webrtc-20170313/ [retrieved: April, 2017]

[5] C. Cramer, K. Kutzner, and T. Fuhrmann, "Bootstrapping locality-aware p2p networks," in Networks, 2004.(ICON 2004). Proceedings. 12th IEEE International Conference on, vol. 1. IEEE, 2004, pp. 357–361.

[6] J. Dinger and O. P. Waldhorst, "Decentralized bootstrapping of p2p systems: a practical view," in NETWORKING 2009. Springer, 2009, pp. 703–715.

[7] S. Dutton, "Webrtc in the real world: Stun, turn and signaling," html5rocks.com, Jul. 2012. [Online]. Available: https://www.html5rocks.com/en/tutorials/webrtc/basics/ [retrieved: April, 2017]

[8] V. Vishnumurthy and P. Francis, "A comparison of structured and unstructured p2p approaches to heterogeneous random peer selection." in Usenix Annual Technical Conference, 2007, pp. 309–322.

[9] E. Adar and B. A. Huberman, "Free riding on gnutella," First monday, vol. 5, no. 10, 2000, pp. 1–22. [Online]. Available: http://firstmonday.org/issues/issue5_10/adar/index.html [Retrieved: April, 2017]

[10] J. Liang, R. Kumar, and K. W. Ross, "Understanding kazaa," Manuscript, Polytechnic Univ, 2004, p. 17.

[11] P. Maymounkov and D. Mazieres, "Kademlia: A peer-to-peer information system based on the xor metric," in Peer-to-Peer Systems. Springer, 2002, pp. 53–65.

[12] I. Stoica, R. Morris, D. Karger, M. F. Kaashoek, and H. Balakrishnan, "Chord: A scalable peer-to-peer lookup service for internet applications," in ACM SIGCOMM Computer Communication Review, vol. 31, no. 4. ACM, 2001, pp. 149–160.

[13] K. Aberer et al., "P-grid: a self-organizing structured p2p system," ACM SIGMOD Record, vol. 32, no. 3, 2003, pp. 29–33.

[14] I. Grigorik, "High performance browser networking," 2013. [Online]. Available: https://hpbn.co/webrtc/ [retrieved: April, 2017]

[15] C. GauthierDickey and C. Grothoff, "Bootstrapping of peer-to-peer networks," in Applications and the Internet, 2008. SAINT 2008. International Symposium on. IEEE, 2008, pp. 205–208.

[16] M. Knoll, A. Wacker, G. Schiele, and T. Weis, "Decentralized bootstrapping in pervasive applications," in Pervasive Computing and Communications Workshops, 2007. PerCom Workshops' 07. Fifth Annual IEEE International Conference on. IEEE, 2007, pp. 589–592.

[17] J. Postel, "Internet Protocol," RFC 791 (INTERNET STANDARD), Internet Engineering Task Force, Sep. 1981, updated by RFCs 1349, 2474, 6864. [Online]. Available: http://www.ietf.org/rfc/rfc791.txt [retrieved: April, 2017]

[18] P. Mahlmann and C. Schindelhauer, Peer-to-Peer-Netzwerke: Algorithmen und Methoden. Springer, Jul. 2007, ISBN: 978-3-540-33992-2.

[19] B. Cohen, "The bittorrent protocol specification," Jan. 2008. [Online]. Available: http://www.bittorrent.org/beps/bep_0003.html [retrieved: April, 2017]

[20] C. Kalt, "Internet Relay Chat: Client Protocol," RFC 2812 (Informational), Internet Engineering Task Force, Apr. 2000. [Online]. Available: http://www.ietf.org/rfc/rfc2812.txt [retrieved: April, 2017]

[21] C. Perkins, M. Westerlund, and J. Ott, "Web real-time communication (webrtc): Media transport and use of rtp," Internet Engineering Task Force, Internet Draft, draft-ietf-rtcweb-rtp-usage-26, Mar. 2016. [Online]. Available: https://tools.ietf.org/html/draft-ietf-rtcweb-rtp-usage-26 [retrieved: April, 2017]

[22] R. Jesup, S. Loreto, and M. Tuexen, "Webrtc data channels," Internet Engineering Task Force, Internet Draft, draft-ietf-rtcweb-data-channel-13, Jan. 2015. [Online]. Available: https://tools.ietf.org/html/draft-ietf-rtcweb-data-channel-13 [retrieved: April, 2017]

[23] J. Postel, "User Datagram Protocol," RFC 768 (INTERNET STANDARD), Internet Engineering Task Force, Aug. 1980. [Online]. Available: http://www.ietf.org/rfc/rfc768.txt [retrieved: April, 2017]

[24] ——, "DoD standard Transmission Control Protocol," RFC 761, Internet Engineering Task Force, Jan. 1980. [Online]. Available: http://www.ietf.org/rfc/rfc761.txt [retrieved: April, 2017]

[25] J. Rosenberg and H. Schulzrinne, "An Offer/Answer Model with Session Description Protocol (SDP)," RFC 3264 (Proposed Standard), Internet Engineering Task Force, Jun. 2002. [Online]. Available: http://www.ietf.org/rfc/rfc3264.txt [retrieved: April, 2017]

[26] M. Handley, H. Schulzrinne, E. Schooler, and J. Rosenberg, "SIP: Session Initiation Protocol," RFC 2543 (Proposed Standard), Internet Engineering Task Force, Mar. 1999. [Online]. Available: http://www.ietf.org/rfc/rfc2543.txt [retrieved: April, 2017]

[27] M. Handley, V. Jacobson, and C. Perkins, "SDP: Session Description Protocol," RFC 4566 (Proposed Standard), Internet Engineering Task Force, Jul. 2006. [Online]. Available: http://www.ietf.org/rfc/rfc4566.txt [retrieved: April, 2017]

[28] H. Schulzrinne, S. Casner, R. Frederick, and V. Jacobson, "RTP: A Transport Protocol for Real-Time Applications," RFC 3550 (INTERNET STANDARD), Internet Engineering Task Force, Jul. 2003. [Online]. Available: http://www.ietf.org/rfc/rfc3550.txt [retrieved: April, 2017]

[29] J. Rosenberg, "Interactive Connectivity Establishment (ICE): A Protocol for Network Address Translator (NAT) Traversal for Offer/Answer Protocols," RFC 5245 (Proposed Standard), Internet Engineering Task Force, Apr. 2010. [Online]. Available: http://www.ietf.org/rfc/rfc5245.txt [retrieved: April, 2017]

[30] J. Rosenberg, R. Mahy, P. Matthews, and D. Wing, "Session Traversal Utilities for NAT (STUN)," RFC 5389 (Proposed Standard), Internet Engineering Task Force, Oct. 2008. [Online]. Available: http://www.ietf.org/rfc/rfc5389.txt [retrieved: April, 2017]

[31] R. Mahy, P. Matthews, and J. Rosenberg, "Traversal Using Relays around NAT (TURN): Relay Extensions to Session Traversal Utilities for NAT (STUN)," RFC 5766 (Proposed Standard), Internet Engineering Task Force, Apr. 2010. [Online]. Available: http://www.ietf.org/rfc/rfc5766.txt [retrieved: April, 2017]

[32] J. Rosenberg, J. Weinberger, C. Huitema, and R. Mahy, "STUN - Simple Traversal of User Datagram Protocol (UDP) Through Network Address Translators (NATs)," RFC 3489 (Proposed Standard), Internet Engineering Task Force, Mar. 2003. [Online]. Available: http://www.ietf.org/rfc/rfc3489.txt [retrieved: April, 2017]

[33] C. Vogt, M. J. Werner, and T. C. Schmidt, "Content-centric user networks: WebRTC as a path to name-based publishing," in Network Protocols (ICNP), 2013 21st IEEE International Conference on, Oct 2013, pp. 1–3.

[34] ——, "Leveraging WebRTC for P2P content distribution in web browsers," in Network Protocols (ICNP), 2013 21st IEEE International Conference on, Oct 2013, pp. 1–2.

[35] D. Boldt and S. Fischer, "Return the Data to the Owner: A Browser-Based Peer-to-Peer Network," The Ninth International Conference on Internet and Web Applications and Services, Jul. 2014, pp. 140–146. [Online]. Available: http://www.thinkmind.org/download.php?articleid=iciw_2014_7_30_20082 [retrieved: April, 2017]

[36] M. J. Werner, C. Vogt, and T. C. Schmidt, "Let our browsers socialize: Building user-centric content communities on webrtc," in Distributed Computing Systems Workshops (ICDCSW), 2014 IEEE 34th International Conference on. IEEE, 2014, pp. 37–44.

[37] C. Desprat, H. Luga, and J.-P. Jessel, "Hybrid client-server and P2P network for web-based collaborative 3D design," in Conference on Computer Graphics, Visualization and Computer Vision, 2015. WSCG 2015. World Society for Computer Graphics, Jun. 215, pp. 229–238.

[38] M. Bu and E. Zhang, "PeerJS – Simple peer-to-peer with WebRTC." [Online]. Available: http://peerjs.com [retrieved: April, 2017]

[39] A. Disterhoft and K. Graffi, "Protected chords in the web: secure p2p framework for decentralized online social networks," in Peer-to-Peer Computing (P2P), 2015 IEEE International Conference on. IEEE, 2015, pp. 1–5.

[40] "Google Web Toolkit." [Online]. Available: http://www.gwtproject.org/ [retrieved: April, 2017]

[41] "OpenChord." [Online]. Available: http://open-chord.sourceforge.net/ [retrieved: April, 2017]

[42] R. J. Bille, Y. Lin, and S. K. Chalup, "Rtcss: a framework for developing real-time peer-to-peer web applications," in Proceedings of the Australasian Computer Science Week Multiconference. ACM, 2016, p. 56.

[43] "Socket.io." [Online]. Available: http://socket.io [retrieved: April, 2017]

[44] P. Mockapetris, "Domain names - concepts and facilities," RFC 1034 (INTERNET STANDARD), Internet Engineering Task Force, Nov. 1987. [Online]. Available: http://www.ietf.org/rfc/rfc1034.txt [retrieved: April, 2017]

[45] T. Brisco, "DNS Support for Load Balancing," RFC 1794 (Informational), Internet Engineering Task Force, Apr. 1995. [Online]. Available: http://www.ietf.org/rfc/rfc1794.txt [retrieved: April, 2017]

[46] "coturn TURN server project." [Online]. Available: https://github.com/coturn/coturn [retrieved: April, 2017]

[47] B. Feher, L. Sidi, A. Shabtai, and R. Puzis, "The security of webrtc," arXiv preprint arXiv:1601.00184, Jan. 2016. [Online]. Available: https://arxiv.org/abs/1601.00184 [retrieved: April, 2017]

[48] R. Arends, R. Austein, M. Larson, D. Massey, and S. Rose, "DNS Security Introduction and Requirements," RFC 4033 (Proposed Standard), Internet Engineering Task Force, Mar. 2005. [Online]. Available: http://www.ietf.org/rfc/rfc4033.txt [retrieved: April, 2017]

[49] "Let's Encrypt – Free SSL/TLS Certificates." [Online]. Available: https://letsencrypt.org/ [retrieved: April, 2017]

[50] R. Barnes, J. Hoffman-Andrews, and K. J., "Automatic Certificate Management Environment (ACME)," Internet Engineering Task Force, Internet Draft, draft-ietf-acme-acme-06, Mar. 2017. [Online]. Available: https://tools.ietf.org/html/draft-ietf-acme-acme-06 [retrieved: April, 2017]

A Study on User-Customized Local Information Notification Service Using Association Analysis

Eunmi Jung, Jooyoung Ko, Andrew G. Kim*, Hyenki Kim
Dept. of Multimedia Engineering
Andong National University, *Appsol.kr INC
Andong, Republic of Korea, *Youngju, Republic of Korea
e-mail: jeilc@naver.com, sonice@anu.ac.kr, geoner@appsol.kr , hkkim@anu.ac.kr (Corresponding Author)

Abstract— **Recently, a vast amount of data is being generated due to the popularization of mobile devices and the increase of various internet services using smart phones. It is necessary to quickly provide the local information needed by the user through filtering of the information in order to satisfy the user's various information needs. Therefore, the study proposes a user-customized local information notification service system based user past history and local resident past history data based on Android. Data used in association analysis is weather information. This study helps users to make quick decision and provide information for making rational choices, and it is helpful for service providers for providing efficient service through user pattern analysis.**

Keywords-Local Information; Big Data; LBS; Association Analysis.

I. INTRODUCTION

Big data refers to a large cluster of data. Social Network Service (SNS) means online service that creates and strengthens social relations through free communication, information sharing, and network expansion among users. The biggest advantage is that anyone can produce content, and deliver content to a large number of people at high speed. As portable mobile devices diversify and network becomes available anytime, anywhere, a large amount of data is created as users use things such as SNS. Also, with the advent of the Internet of things, data is being generated from individuals or objects anytime and anywhere. These large amounts of big data are now recognized as important assets and it can be analyzed and reworked to produce meaningful information [1].

Association analysis is the process of finding association rules between items that exist between data. It analyzes the relationship of specific rules that appear when a user purchases a product or uses a service to provide better products or services to the user [2]. This study aims to provide users with customized local information by analyzing the relationship between user past history and local resident past history with weather. The aim is to analyze weather factors based on restaurant information and provide a recommendation list for users to select restaurants according to the current weather. Another aim is to provide users with quick recognition of restaurants that were frequently chosen by users through visualization. With the spread of various mobile devices, it is possible to use smartphones regardless of age and living area. In Korea, it is not difficult to use wired and wireless communication in rural as well as urban areas due to the development of network environment. This study is a system design that provides local information service more quickly through 'Associations Analysis' with user history, local history and weather. It is determined that the user-customized recommendation service user interface helps a user to make rational selections.

The structure of this paper is as follows. Session 2 describes the related studies, Session 3 describes the design of customized local information notification service, and Session 4 describes the conclusion of the paper.

II. RELATED STUDIES

There are a variety of efforts from companies and service providers to provide better products and services for consumers. Data mining is required to find association rules in various data [3]. Users register their experiences such as product reviews on Internet boards after using products and services, and these contents have been analyzed and applied to developing products and services. This is a product and service improvement method based on user experience. User experience is a concept that includes the overall experience, such as the emotional response, value, and attitude that users experience when using a product or service [4]. The study by Hwang used big data analysis to study a user experience evaluation methodology focusing on analysis of online reviews of Amazon Echo [5].

Among the analysis methods of big data, association analysis is a method of finding the association rule between the items existing in the data and figuring out the purchase characteristics of the customer. By analyzing the structured and unstructured data generated by customers using products and services, products and services that are right for the customers can be suggested in advance. The study "Spatial Association Analysis among Seoul Metropolitan Cities" by Park, analyzed the spatial association between Seoul metropolitan cities after the 1990s to provide basic data to support policy establishment [6].

In the case of application using Big Data, there is an example of solving the difficulties of citizens in Seoul by operating a night bus in areas with a lot of nighttime floating population. As a result of analyzing big data, using mobile phones, from midnight to early morning in March 2013, the bus route was improved by analyzing patterns of traffic demand and flow population in a specific area [7]. In Japan, the Nomura Research Institute has used a smartphone navigation service to minimize the damage to road traffic in the 2011 Great East Japan Earthquake [8].

In Park 's study, it was found that affinities, information, and reciprocity influence brand awareness in mobile advertising through Location Based Service (LBS) mobile location - based advertising [9]. Also, the study by Jung analyzed the sales data of restaurants to analyze the relationship with sales. She found that the number of times a consumer visits a restaurant is affected by variables such as weather, holiday and newspaper articles, and that weather affects restaurant sales [10]. The research in has been conducted to provide users with frequent location information and personal recommendation services through their location information and usage histories [11]. The purpose of this study is to analyze the relationship with the weather in choosing restaurants and to provide recommended restaurants to help the customer select a restaurant menu using weather variables. This study not only helps consumers to select a restaurant, but also analyzes the characteristics of purchases in restaurants in the area, and in the perspective of the vendor, it can help provide the right food for the consumers by analyzing the characteristics of the buyers.

III. USER CUSTOMIZED LOCAL INFORMATION NOTIFICATION SERVICE DESIGN

The system designed in the study makes it possible to provide local information notification service based on Android by using past user history, past history data of local residents and weather information. Figure 1 is a conceptual diagram of a customized local information notification service system.

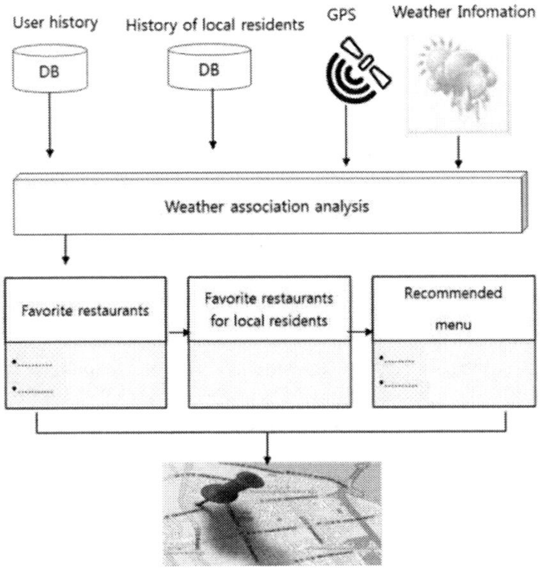

Figure 1. System conceptual Diagram

The data used in the study include past user history, past history data of local residents, and weather information uses cloudiness and precipitation to classify into clear, overcast, rain, and snow. Past user history is used to show the list of restaurants that the user often visited in relation to today's weather through association analysis with the weather. Also, a list of surrounding restaurants that match user menus frequently searched by residents is created, a list of surrounding restaurants where residents most often take deliveries is created, and menus the local residents often order in relation to the weather is also recommended. In addition it is a service that visualizes the related data on the map. Figure 2(a) shows data obtained from analysis of past user history and association analysis with the weather, and it is a screen that shows a list of restaurants frequently visited by the user. When the menu is selected, it is directly linked to order. Figure 2(b) shows a screen visualizing a list of restaurants that local residents frequently visit based on current location.

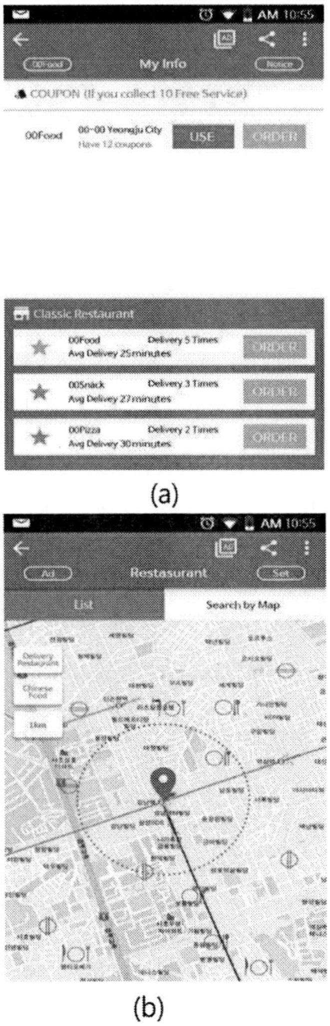

Figure 2. Favorite restaurants and single stree map

Figure 3(a) is a screen that shows user –related recommended menu lists when a restaurant is selected. Figure 3(b) shows the selected final restaurant order screen. 'Jajangmyeon' is a Korean food name and Noodles with Black Soybean Sauce

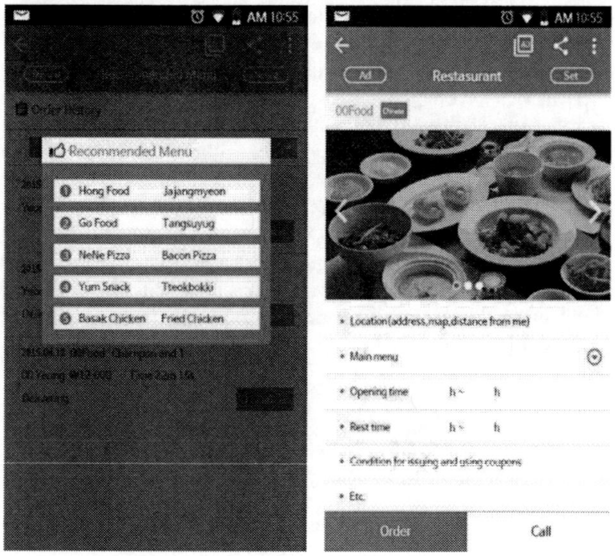

(a) (b)

Figure 3.Menu recommendation and ordering UI

Table 1 is a table of major associations extracted for association analysis. To analyze whether food is associated with the weather, we analyzed it using the 'arules' library of the R programming language.

TABLE 1. MAJOR ASSOCIATIONS EXTRACTION

lhs		rhs	support	confidence	lift
{}	=>	{jajangmyeon}	0.533333	0.5333333	1
{rain}	=>	{jajangmyeon}	0.444444	0.8333333	1.086957
{sun}	=>	{naengmyeon}	0.444444	0.5797101	1.086957

As a result of extracting major associations, it was confirmed that "rain" was 53% within the total, and in the case where "rain" and "jajangmyeon" appeared at the same time, it was 44% of the total. The effect of "rain" on "jajangmyeon" was found to be 83%, which confirmed a very high association.

IV. CONCLUSION

Local information refers to all information relevant to the corresponding community, and 'local information service' refers to a service that provides this everyday and practical local information. The study provided a customized local information notification service through association analysis between weather and delivery food to help quick decision-making in users and provision of efficient service by businesses. Through the study, it was possible to analyze restaurant order characteristics in a region and businesses can analyze purchase patterns to aid in providing user customized service.

ACKNOWLEDGMENT

This work was supported by a grant from 2016 Joint-industry-academic Research Fund of SMBA, Korea.

REFERENCES

[1] K. Bok, and J. Yoo, "Activation Policy and Case Study of Big Data", Journal of Electrical Engineering & Technology, Information and Communications Magazine, Vol. 31, No.11, pp.3-13, 2014.

[2] T. Brijs, G. Swinnen, K. Vanhoof, and G. Wets, "Using Association Rules for Product Assortment Decisions: A Case Study, KDD", '99 Proceedings of the fifth ACM SIGKDD international conference on Knowledge discovery and data mining, Aug. 2013, pp. 254-260 , ISSN 1-58113-143-7

[3] B. Liu, W. Hsu, and Y. Ma, "Integrating Classification and Association Rule Mining", Appeared in KDD-98, New York, Aug. 1998, pp. 27-31, ISBN 978-1-57735-004-0

[4] K. Lee, I. Lee, S. Jun, S. Yang, G. Choi, J. Kim, S. Park, and M. Han, "How to Measure the User Experience?", Proceeding of HCI KOREA 2016: The HCI Society of Korea, Vol. 2, pp. 851-856, 2008.

[5] H. Hwang, H. Shim, and J. Choi, "Exploration of User Experience Research Method with Big Data Analysis : Focusing on the Online Review Analysis of Echo", The Journal of the Korea Contents Association, Vol. 16, No. 8, 2016.

[6] J. Park, H. Chang, and J. Kim, "Spatial Association of Population Concentration in Seoul Metropolitan Area" Journal of The Korean Society of Civil Engineers D, Vol. 22, No. 3D, pp391-397, 2008.

[7] Seoul, Seoul, Big Data Usage Speed Analysis, [Online]. Available from: http://opengov.seoul.go.kr/section/1520565, 2014.05.12.

[8] Y. M. Yoon, "Big Data Global 10 Best Practices Big Data – Lead the world with Big Data", National Informmation Society Agency, 2012.

[9] C. Park, "The Impact of LBS Mobile Advertising on the Brand Marketing," Korea Real Estate Society, Vol. 33, No. 1, pp. 391-409, 2015.

[10] E. Jung, "A Study on Prediction Service Modeling Using Big Data", Ph. D. Dissertation, Andong National University, December, 2016.

[11] E. Jung, J. Ko, and H. Kim, "Design of Customized Local Information System Based on Big Data Analysis", International Journal of Applied Engineering Research, Vol. 11, No. 2, pp. 766-769, 2016.

A Study on the WAI-ARIA of Domestic Websites with High Session in Korea

Chorong Kim
Dept. of Multimedia Engineering,
Andong National University
Andong, Republic of Korea
e-mail: chfhd7379@naver.com

Eunju Park
Dept. of Multimedia Engineering,
Andong National University
Andong, Republic of Korea
e-mail: eunju@anu.ac.kr

Hankyu Lim
Dept. of Multimedia Engineering,
Andong National University
Andong, Republic of Korea
e-mail: hklim@anu.ac.kr

***Abstract*—Web accessibility depends on the development of universally accessible web content. The World Wide Web Consortium (W3C) has implemented many regulations for the improvement of web accessibility, and compliance with these regulations ensures that everyone will have equal access to web contents. HyperText Markup Language 5 (HTML5), which has been recently adopted as the web standard, also contains elements that support accessibility. Current web pages do not only depend on HTML and Cascading Style Sheet (CSS), but they also use various kinds of dynamic contents based on Rich Internet Applications (RIA). Therefore, HTML5 specifies the Web Accessibility Initiative-Accessible Rich Internet Application (WAI-ARIA) to improve accessibility of web applications, including RIA components. In this paper, the usability and accessibility of WAI-ARIA is evaluated targeting the top 50 websites accessed by most domestic users. According to the results, 78% of domestic websites have not applied the WAI-ARIA and only 6% have used it correctly.**

Keywords-HTML5; Web; Web Accessibility; WAI-ARIA; Mobile Accessibility; Web Standard; User Interface

I. INTRODUCTION

Along with the rapid growth of the Internet, there have been a number of developments in the status of almost all fields, including politics, economics, society, culture, and administration. The quality of private lives can be enriched through the various digital cultures found on the Internet. However, informational discrimination can occur among individuals who are not familiar with or are unable to use the Internet [1][2]. Thus, it is important to create web content that guarantees accessibility for those with cognitive impairment or visual, hearing, or neuropathological disorders.

The Web Accessibility Initiative (WAI) of the World Wide Web Consortium (W3C) has established various standards and relevant guidelines [1] to improve web accessibility. Web standards are to be coded according to specifications and exclude private markup so that content can be operated on most browsers [3]. Therefore, coding regulations that comply with web standards allow everyone to equally and easily use information found on the Web without alienation due to various access issues [4].

HyperText Markup Language 5 (HTML5) was accepted as the final W3C standard on October 28, 2014 [5]. This new standard includes components supporting improvements to web content accessibility [6][7]. The Accessible Rich Internet Application (ARIA), which was newly added to HTML5, defines accessibility enhancement methods for disabled individuals, when web contents and applications are produced using asynchronous JavaScript and XML (Ajax) and JavaScript. In HTML5, the Web Accessibility Initiative-Accessible Rich Internet Application (WAI-ARIA) specification enhances the accessibility of web applications [8][9].

Most current web pages do not only provide simple contents created using HTML and Cascading Style Sheet (CSS), but also dynamic contents using new methods, such as JavaScript. Despite the increased use of dynamic contents, no official method has been implemented to evaluate their accessibility [10]. Since 2015, W3C has provided "ARIA Validator" to evaluate the accessibility of dynamic contents. In this paper, therefore, WAI-ARIA, which was specified to substantiate the web application accessibility of HTML5, is evaluated to determine if it has been properly applied. To this end, the top 50 websites accessed by most domestic users during the first half of 2016 were selected and tested for their accessibility according to WAI-ARIA. An automatic evaluation method, the ARIA Validator provided by the W3C, was applied. According to the evaluation result, 39 (78%) out of the 50 websites tested were not using WAI-ARIA. Only 3 websites (6%), received a "Pass" rating for the accessibility test, and 8 (16%) websites received a "Fail." Although many recent websites use dynamic contents, few of them use WAI-ARIA correctly. Thus, Web users with disabilities and/or disorders have difficulty approaching dynamic contents in many of the web pages. As Internet usage increases and more information is gathered, it should be equally available to all. Therefore, in order to make improvements, web developers and all relevant personnel should make an effort to modify their understanding and improve web accessibility.

This paper's construction goes like this. In chapter two, we introduced studies about web accessibility, accessibility supporting elements of the HTML5, entrance background and use of WAI-ARIA, ARIA validator, etc. In chapter three, we did ARIA validator evaluation of domestic websites from the top 50 high session websites in Korea and analyzed the result. Finally in chapter four, we described our conclusion and assignment from now on.

II. RELATED RESEARCH

Web emphasizes universality, and use of the web directly affects the quality of life in contemporary society. As web content and websites have become more application-oriented, rich internet application technology has appeared, improving user experience (UX) on websites. However, it has also become a factor making the maintenance of accessibility to websites difficult and making usage of the web by the disabled more difficult. Web Accessibility Initiative-Accessible Rich Internet Applications, an accessibility guideline for RIA, provides effective accessibility to web content and web applications.

A. *Web Accessibility*

The power of the Web originates from its universality, and equal access for all people is its most important component [4]. In modern society, the Web is closely connected to human life and it expands to most areas; web accessibility is regarded as a necessary component for everyone, including those with various disabilities.

Web accessibility implies the development of web content that can be accessed by everyone regardless of their abilities or disabilities. Web accessibility means that everyone is guaranteed the right and opportunity to make use of services offered on websites, irrespective of physical and technical conditions and the user's knowledge [11]. Therefore, web contents should be created so that everyone can recognize, operate, and understand them [12].

Web standards and regulations are defined by the WAI of the W3C, and are related to web technology. Websites that comply with web standards enhance accessibility.

B. *Accessibility Supporting Elements of the HTML5*

The web standard HTML4 was specified in December 1999. The new standard, HTML5, was specified in October 2014; it targets and follows web application development, breaking the boundaries of the pre-existing HTML concept. HTML5 contains components intended to improve accessibility [13].

The specifications for HTML5 are provided by WAI-ARIA, which has been defined by the WAI of the W3C to improve the accessibility of web content [7]. HTML5 has advantages that are compatible with all browsers and platforms and can be applied to various devices [6]. The accessibility support elements of HTML5 include Semantic Structure, canvas, audio, video, and WAI-ARIA. The semantic components <head>, <footer>, and <section> clarify the structural meaning of the document. The input form can be validated by the browser.

C. *Entrance Background and Use of WAI-ARIA*

Web content storage methods have evolved from coding skills based on HTML to RIA methods. Most web accessibility standards have evolved to include RIA content, such as interactive web contents containing JavaScript code, Flash, and Flex [10]. Contents that are produced by the RIA method provide dynamic and splendid User Experience (UX). However, there is a problem in that disabled individuals who depend on the use of assistive devices such as screen readers cannot use web applications created using RIA techniques [14]. In the case of web applications created using JavaScript or Ajax, such assistive techniques cannot accurately understand the meaning of a component that was manufactured in factors that do not have a certain meaning, such as <div> or <span>. Hence, W3C announced WAI-ARIA, aiming to improve universal accessibility to web contents and the Web.

WAI-ARIA is extremely helpful in developing applications using JavaScript and Ajax. Its role and areas of application are already supported by many screen readers, and it can be utilized to improve accessibility on subsidiary devices. With WAI-ARIA, one can add role, property, and state to the web application [7]. Table 1 shows the properties and examples of WAI-ARIA [9]. "Role" defines the function of a certain factor. It can provide a clear definition of its function—whether the area is a navigation area, a button, or a title. "Property" indicates the property or situation of each factor. For example, it lets users understand whether an input box of a form is read-only, required, or auto-complete. "State" shows the current status of a factor and it has values according to change. For example, it shows whether a menu is expanded, whether an invalid value was input, or whether contents are hidden. The use of these functions can improve the accessibility and usability of web applications.

TABLE I. WAI-ARIA ATTRIBUTES

Attribute	Example	Explanation
role	<a href= "#" onclick= "play()" role= "button">	Screen reader reads a factor as a button instead of link.
property	<input type= "password" id= "user_pw" aria-required= "true">	Thanks to the property of aria-required= "true," users know that the corresponding item is essential in the screen reader.
state	<div role= "item" aria-expanded= "false">	Statement of aria-expanded="false" lets users know that it is currently folded.

D. *ARIA Validator*

The ARIA Validator is a program that was produced by Rick Brown in April 2015; it inspects WAI-ARIA implementation issues. It can evaluate code in the form of a web browser extension and be extended on the Chrome browser. The ARIA Validator is on the W3C web page introducing various evaluation tools related to web accessibility [15].

Figures 1 and 2 show the results of inspections of random websites using the ARIA Validator, indicating the URL of the evaluated webpage, evaluation time, and results of the "Roles Validated." Figure 1 shows the results without any ARIA roles.

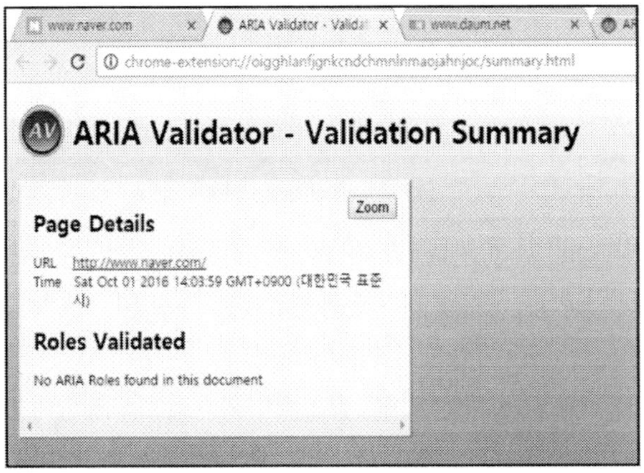

Figure 1. ARIA Validator Testing Result Screen (no ARIA role)

Figure 2 shows the test result for an ARIA that was incorrectly applied to a web page. Such pages are given a "Fail" rating and a link is given to sample pages that explain the correct usage. The page in Figure 2 indicates both correctly and incorrectly used ARIAs. While "button," "region," "search," "combobox," and "alertdialog" correctly applied ARIA, the application is incorrect in the case of several "comboboxes." Thus, the rating achieved is "Fail." When users select the spread menu for the "Fail" factor, they are able to see an explanation.

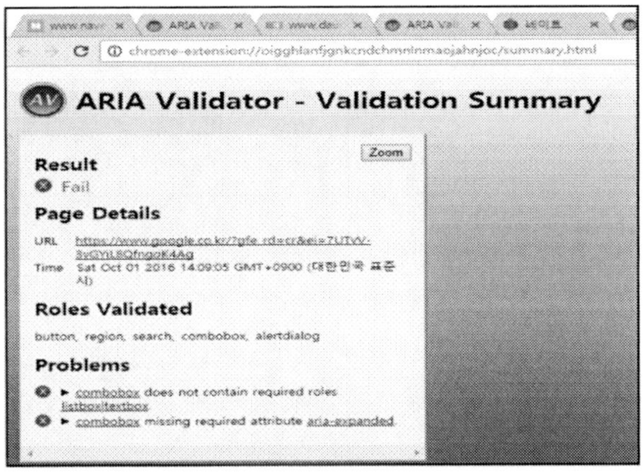

Figure 2. ARIA Validator Testing Result Screen (Fail)

III. ARIA VALIDATOR EVALUATION OF DOMESTIC WEBSITES FROM THE TOP 50 HIGH SESSION WEBSITES IN KOREA

In this paper, applying the ARIA Validator for targeting, the accessibility of WAI-ARIA was evaluated on the top 50 websites most accessed by domestic users. Target websites were selected from the rankings of March 2016 at "ranky.com," which evaluates and explains web and mobile sites [16]. The ARIA Validator evaluation was executed on October 1, 2016.

The graph in Figure 3 illustrates the number of websites that did and did not use HTML5 in their construction in March and October of 2016.

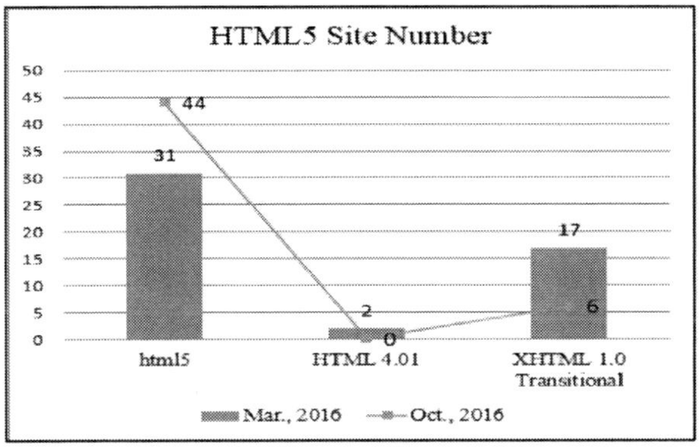

Figure 3. HTML5 Building Site Numbers

The HTML5 standardization process stresses accessibility and includes ways to enhance it. Therefore, accessibility factors that were not previously considered in earlier versions can be used in websites that are built using HTML5. As such, HTML5 helps to establish websites with improved accessibility. The results show that in October 2016, 44 out of 50 websites had been constructed using HTML5 and only 6 websites had not been based on HTML5. This is a higher ratio than that obtained for March 2016 when 31 out of 50 websites had been based on HTML5.

Figure 4 is a graph describing the research results for WAI-ARIA accessibility using the ARIA Validation targeting the top 50 websites accessed by most domestic users in October 2016. Among 50 websites, 39 (78%) were marked as "No ARIA roles found in this document," which means the developers did not use WAI-ARIA. WAI-ARIA is supported in HTML5, so that 6 websites that did not use HTML5 also did not use WAI-ARIA. Eleven websites applied WAI-ARIA, but 8 of them rated a "Fail." Only 3 websites—"nate," "kakao," and "epost" rated a "Pass." According to the evaluation result, the majority of domestic websites had not used WAI-ARIA and most of the websites using WAI-ARIA applied it incorrectly. This implies that although new HTML5 standards are being used, the perception of accessibility is low. Currently, many dynamic contents are in use and improvements are necessary to allow users to access certain web pages; developers should make efforts to change their mindsets.

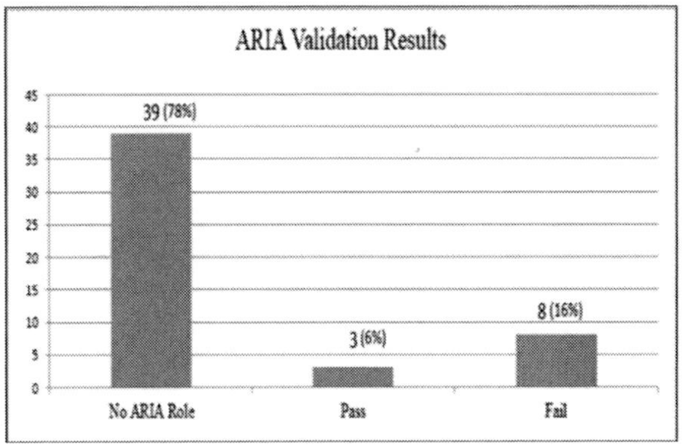

Figure 4. ARIA Validation Results

TABLE II. ANALYSIS OF PASS SITES

Site	Pass Element	Used Tag
nate	banner, search, navigation	<div id= "NateBi" class= "area_bi" **role= "banner"**> <div class= "area_search" **role= "search"**> <div id= "divGnb" class="area_gnb" **role="navigation"**>
kakao	dialog	<div aria-hidden= "true" aria-labelledby= "urgent_notice_modal_label" class= "modal fade" id= "urgent_notice_modal" **role= "dialog"** tabindex= "-1">
epost	main	<div class= "slider" **role="main"**>

Table 2 shows the websites that achieved a "Pass" with the ARIA Validation. Among the 50 websites, only 3 (6%) rated a "Pass"—"nate," "kakao," and "epost." "Nate" described the "banner," "search," and "navigation" components using the WAI-ARIA role. Also implemented with the WAI-ARIA role were "dialog" of "kakao" and "main" of "epost." In the cases of "nate" and "epost," however, pages other than the main page had not applied WAI-ARIA. Moreover, although the use ARIA is required for many website factors, ARIA is clearly stated in the case of only a few of the factors. The "nate" website has a clear ARIA statement in only 3 out of 227 <div> factors. Analysis of the source in the actual website indicated the necessity for correcting ARIA use.

Table 3 shows "Example of Fail Message" and "Roles Validated" for websites that received "Fail" in the ARIA Validation test results. "Roles Validated" shows the factors that correctly used ARIA.

"Example of Fail Message" shows the factors that incorrectly used ARIA. "Google" correctly used ARIA for a number of factors; however, it did not use ARIA in the case of several factor attributes that are related to ARIA among

TABLE III. ANALYSIS OF FAIL SITES

	Example of Fail Message	Roles Validated
Google	- combobox does not contain required roles listbox |textbox - combobox missing required attribute aria-expanded.	button, region, search, combobox, alert, dialog
Facebook	- aria-required is not allowed when "an exactly equivalent native attribute is available"	presentation, main, alert, button, contentinfo
Youtube	- heading unsupported attribute aria-selected - link unsupported attribute aria-selected - menuitem not in required scope menu|menubar	alert, link, navigation, menu, menuitem, complementary, main. Button, dialog
Bing	- listbox does not contain required roles option - aria-expanded is not supported on this element - aria-owns IDREF off_menu_cont must not be "aria-owned" by more than one element (repeated 2 more times)	search, combobox, listbox, navigation, group, complementary, button, contentinfo
Twitter	- textbox unsupported attribute aria-expanded - textbox unsupported attribute aria-expanded	search, listbox, presentation, option, group, button, textbox
Msn	- menu does not contain required rolesgroup|menuitemradio|menuitem|menuitemcheckbox|menuitemradio - aria-expanded is not supported on this element	banner, search, menu, main, menubar, menuitem, button, complementary, contentinfo
Yonhapnews	- button unsupported attribute aria-selected. - button unsupported attribute aria-selected.	button, slider
Microsoft	- menu does not contain required rolesgroup|menuitemradio|menuitem|menuitemcheckbox|menuitemradio - menu does not contain required rolesgroup|menuitemradio|menuitem|menuitemcheckbox|menuitemradio	banner, navigation, menubar, button, menu, search, main, region, radiogroup, radio, contentinfo

the HTML sources of "fail" "combobox," including <input class= "gsfi lst-d-f" id= "lst-ib" name= "q" autocomplete= "off" aria-label= "search" aria-haspopup= "false" role= "combobox" aria-autocomplete= "both">. For more accurate information, the ARIA Validator requires a mark on whether it is a listbox or textbox and a clear statement on the spread menu (aria-expand). It is possible to accurately define the role and the status of the combobox of <input role= "listbox" aria-expand= "true">.

IV. CONCLUSION

Tim Berners-Lee, the inventor of the World Wide Web, said that "the power of the Web lies in generality and providing Web accessibility to everyone regardless of disabilities" [16]. The Web is being increasingly used by many, including public organizations, as a means of receiving and disseminating information. Therefore, individuals with disabilities should be guaranteed the same level of Web accessibility as able-bodied people.

Due to the increase in dynamic contents, the factors that support their accessibility have been in classified in HTML5. However, it was proven that not many websites build their web pages supporting accessibility according to classifications. Although HTML5 was widely used in a number of websites before its designation as a standard, there were only a few websites in our study that used WAI-ARIA. Constructing websites that comply with accessibility regulations can be burdensome to web developers. However, considering that accessibility defines the basic spirit of the Web, the development of websites that comply with accessibility standards is deserving of developers' efforts and interest. In future work, we will investigate the ARIA compliance rate for international web pages and continue to work on ways to increase the accessibility of dynamic contents. In order to know the relationship between the pages with RIA and web accessibility, we will research the web accessibility evaluation for both the pages using the WAI-ARIA and the pages not using the pages not using the WAI-ARIA.

ACKNOWLEDGMENT

This research was supported by a grant from 2017 Seoul Accord Project (2011-0-00559) of MISP (Ministry of Science, ICT and Future Planning) and IITP (Institute for Information and Communication Technology Promotion).

REFERENCES

[1] SeongJe Park and SeokChan Jeong, "The Comparative Analysis of Web Accessibility Evaluation Tools by Evaluating Image Contents on the Web Pages," The e-Business Studies, Vol. 11, No. 3, pp. 347-366, 2010.

[2] HeonSik Joo, "A Study on Web accessibility situation of Public Institution and Major IT Companies Institutions," Journal of the Korea Society of Computer and Information, Vol. 14, No. 10, pp. 175-187, 2009.

[3] Jim. Thatcher and Michael. R. Burks, "Web accessibility & web standards and regulatory compliance," Acorn Publishing Co, 2011.

[4] SeungHwan Gu, KyongSok An, KwangMo Lee, and SungJin Choi, "Implementation of a Research Task Management System for Support Smart Work Considering Web Accessibility," Journal of the Korea Contents Association, Vol. 13, No. 9, pp. 39-48, 2013.

[5] W3C Recommendation, http://www.w3.org/TR/html5/ [retrieved: 10, 2016]

[6] HongGi Cha, WonSuk Lee, and SeungYun Lee, "W3C HTML5 Standardization Trend," (ICT Standard & Certification) TTA Journal, Vol. 159, pp. 94-101, 2015.

[7] Shiraishi Shunpei, "Introduction to HTML5 & API," Freelec in Republic of Korea, 2010.

[8] Mozilla Developer Network, https://developer.mozilla.org/ko/docs/Web/Accessibility/ARIA [retrieved: 10, 2016]

[9] Brian P. Hogan, "HTML5 & CSS3," Insight in Republic of Korea, 2011.

[10] Hawoong Han, "An Assessment Method of Web Accessibility for RIA Contents," Graduate School of Information Sciences, Soongsil University, 2011.

[11] KyoungSoon Hong, "A Study on Improvements of Automatic Web Accessibility Evaluation Tool Using Empirical Knowledge," Doctorate thesis from Graduate School of Department of Information and Telecommunication Engineering, Incheon National University, 2015.

[12] Korea Web Accessibility Evaluation Center, http://www.kwacc.or.kr/WebAccessibility/Definition [retrieved: 10, 2016]

[13] W3c Web Accessibility Initiative, https://www.w3.org/WAI/PF/html-task-force [retrieved: 10, 2016]

[14] National Information Society Agency, "WAI-ARIA," National Information Society Agency, 2016.

[15] W3C Web Accessibility initiative, https://www.w3.org/WAI/ER/tools, [retrieved: 10, 2016]

[16] Rankey.com, http://www.rankey.com [retrieved: 03, 2016]

The Contradictions of Social Media Crowdsourcing in Crises Management of War-torn Societies

Khaled Saleh Al Omoush
Associate Professor
Al-Zaytoonah University of Jordan
Amman-Jordan
email: k.Alomoush@zuj.edu.jo

***Abstract*— This research aims to investigate the contradictions of social media crowdsourcing in crisis management in war-torn societies incorporating five intrinsic paradoxes. These contradictions were derived from the literature and practices of social media crowdsourcing in Syria. It concluded that these contradictions represent profound influential factors on the value of social media crowdsourcing in such crises. The identification and analysis of such contradictions enhances the efforts of reinforcing the positive interactions and diminishing the negative practices to support the value of social media crowdsourcing in crisis management. Furthermore, the research presents technical and ethical solutions to enhance the participation value of social media crowdsourcing.**

Keywords—social media crowdsourcing; usefulness; call for peace; wisdom; truth; sense of community.

I. INTRODUCTION

Social media has become an integral part of people's daily lives. It has provided an unprecedented opportunity and preferred platform to communicate and collaborate [1]. Furthermore, it has been widely adopted in voluntary organizations as a means to create civic engagement and organize collective actions [2]. Recent emergencies and crises have shown the positive impact of using social media in the collective crises management [3].

Several studies [1][4][5] emphasizes the role of social computing and the advances in social media in empowering the concept of crowdsourcing. Crowdsourcing is a combination of the words outsourcing and crowd [6]. The term first appeared in 2006 to describe the act of taking a job traditionally performed by a designated agent and outsourcing it to an undefined group of people [7][8]. Crowdsourcing has emerged as an efficient way to solve a wide range of tasks [9]. However, previous research [10][11] confirmed that crowdsourcing is enabled only through the technology of the web including social media. Events of the current civil wars in the Middle East are showing new kinds of powerful crisis communities, which are made possible by new social media that supports crowdsourcing approaches.

In war-torn societies, social media crowdsourcing is tightly connected to the off-line society. It not only facilitates the integration of the offline and online environments, but also fosters on-the-ground activities. The antagonism and differences between and within the crowds become problematic when social media crowdsourcing is used to participate in crisis management in war-torn societies. In fact, it is the mirror of off-line contradictions. Usually, the crowd of war-torn society is not unified but is rather drawn in different crowds including loyalists, opponents and pacifists that are made up of different ethnic and religious subcrowds. The perception of social media crowdsourcing effects cannot be understood in isolation from the reasons of using it [5]. The literature has provided different fundamental explanations for the motivations of social media crowdsourcing. In contrast, crowdsourcing is encountering a wide range of risks and ambiguities resulting in contradictions that are derived from the syncretism of crowds that participate in crisis management, and from the decoupling that can be operated when such efforts are implemented on the social media. Such contradictions embedded in the social media crowdsourcing might harm crisis management efforts threatening the life and safety of people.

Resolving these contradictions became the challenge of crisis management stakeholders. Understanding such contradictions in a helpfully and ethically responsible manner is essential [7]. The current civil wars prove that the operators of social media services share the citizens of such societies the challenges of maximizing the value of social media crowdsourcing through minimizing contradictions in the practices of crowds. Furthermore, the investigation of crowdsourcing contradictions helps understand the structure of the online communities, which can connect to on-the-ground activities [4]. The analysis of these contradictions enhances the efforts of reinforcing the positive interactions and diminishing the negative practices to support the value of social media crowdsourcing in crisis management.

Based on the aforementioned discussion, the purpose of this research is to investigate the contradictions and their impact on participation value of social media crowdsourcing in crisis management in war-torn societies. Based on the previous literature review and following up on the Syrian crisis via social media, the present research has derived five intrinsic paradoxes. Furthermore, the research presents technical and ethical solutions to enhance the participation value of social media crowdsourcing in crisis management. The reminder of this paper is organized as follows: Section II provides a review of the literature research, which has been published in the subject area of social media crowdsourcing in crises situations. Section III presents the research model and the respective constructs. Finally, section IV concludes and outlines the future work.

II. LITERATURE REVIEW

Crowdsourcing can be described as an umbrella term for a set of tools and techniques that deal with the process of outsourcing work to large and possibly unknown groups of people [9]. In fact, disasters and crises are areas where crowdsourcing is having a real impact [4].

A review of the current literature reveals that the recent research on social media crowdsourcing in crises situations can be classified into three major categories. A considerable stream of research [2][4][5] was oriented to investigate the role of social media crowdsourcing in crisis management. It is worth mentioning that most of these studies has been dedicated to develop different crowdsourcing applications to involve the crowds in the crises management employing the unique capabilities of social media. The literature review also revealed that many of recent studies [1][12] investigated the role of social media crowdsourcing in generating and using big data during disasters and emergencies. A significant stream of research [7][12][13] intended to study different issues on the response to crises through the use and analysis of big data. The third category of literature included considerable body of research [14][15][16] conducted to determine motivations and uses of social media crowdsourcing via Mobile during disasters and crises. In this regard, a considerable body of research (e.g., [17][18]) has been conducted to investigate the role of social media in the efforts of search, rescue, and emergency response.

It is worth mentioning that the vast majority of previous studies addressed the topic of social media crowdsourcing in terms of natural disasters and short-term human-made emergencies and crises, such as terrorist attacks. Furthermore, they have revolved around the existence of a wide range of authorities, such as police, fire, emergency medical and other governmental authorities that can be relied upon to coordinate the efforts of emergency and crisis management. In such cases, people directly affected by the crisis are often excluded from information processing and interpretation, and marginalized in subsequent response decision-making that affect their very lives [13]. In addition, most of the aforementioned studies proposed that the social media crowd is unified.

Although there is an extensive and evolving interest in the role of social media crowdsourcing in crises management, study on contradictions of online crowds' practices is still very limited and no study had been undertaken to examine the contradictions of social media crowdsourcing in crises management of war-torn societies. Additional efforts for understanding this contradictions are worthwhile.

III. RESEARCH MODEL

The research model has two main tasks, including diagnoses contradictions and proposing solutions to them. The investigation of contradictions embedded in the social media crowdsourcing during civil wars seeks to identify possibilities for capturing the positive practices and diminishing the negative practices associated with it in order to support the value of social media crowdsourcing in crisis management. However, the research model represented in Figure 1 proposes that, during large-scale and long-term crises that arise out of civil wars, the participation in crisis management via social media crowdsourcing incorporates a number of contradictions in the practices of crowds. These contradictions represent profound influential factors on the value of social media crowdsourcing in such crises conditions.

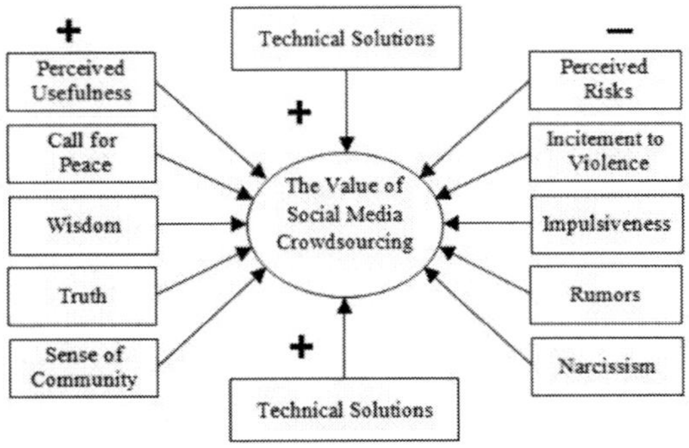

Figure 1. The research model

The present research suggests two main solutions, that can be classified into ethical and technical solutions. This is to minimize the negative impact of such contradictions on the efforts of participating in crisis management via social media crowdsourcing. Based on the previous literature review and following up on the crowds of civil wars on social media in the Syrian crisis, the present study has derived the contradictions as shown in Table I.

TABLE I. CONTRADICTIONS OF SOCIAL MEDIA CROWDSOURCING

+	References	−	References
Perceived Usefulness	[3][5][14]	Perceived Risks	[16]-[23]
Call for Peace	[3][5][25]	Incitement to Violence	[24] - [26]
Wisdom	[8][27][28]	Impulsiveness	[10][15][30]
Truth	[3][5][12]	Rumors	[23][30][31]
Sense of Community	[14][26][34]	Narcissism	[35]-[38]

Below, is a more detailed discussion of each dimension research model. Later on, the research presents technical and ethical solutions to enhance the participation value of social media crowdsourcing in crisis management.

A. The Value of Social Media Crowdsourcing

The convergence of social computing has generated new horizons to explore and use the capabilities of social media crowdsourcing in the humanitarian crises, especially those associated with armed conflicts in the civil war-torn societies. With the absence of governmental institutions, millions of people are still steadfast in their country and struggling to survive using all means available. In such case, citizens have only themselves to rely on, coping with unpredictable events, and encouraging each other to stay in their homes in spite of the risks. In such situations the collaboration of citizens is becoming more and more indispensable, where citizens are moving from a reactive behavior to a proactive outlook characterized by free involvement and self-responsibility [2][3]. In such large-scale and long-term crises, one of the greatest challenges to those involved in crisis management efforts, including citizens, is to have efficient, stable, and accessible tele-communication platforms for reaching a large amount of people on a limited amount of time and resources [2][3][4].

The effectiveness of social media tools, including SNSs, image and video hosting sites, Wikis, and blogs, has been increasing in every area of human life in recent years [5]. In the past few years, the initial role of social media as a means to keep in touch with friends, family and colleagues has evolved and they are becoming a more important means of communication and collaboration during emergencies, disasters, and crises [6]. Nowadays, Syrians are employing are employing social media crowdsourcing effectively in exchanging, disseminating, and sharing information, solutions, and advices on how to deal with the different and complex features of the crisis. These features include securing the basic human needs, such as foods, drinkable water, emergency medical centers and necessary medications, fuel, and identifying the sources and places of their availability. They also include identifying the safe places and roads and early warning for new conflict hot spots. Mobile social networking has also provided an interactive platform to transfer the public needs, trends, opinions, and mood to the different parties of the crisis and promote the reconciliations and settlements between all parties. They are playing a vital role in transferring the truth of events, hardship, miseries, tribulations of humans under this crisis to the outside world, and reuniting refigure families, and following up the affairs of missing and abducted persons. In Syrian case, it has been of great value for Syrians and the world to satisfy the need to have the latest and unique information available during crises. The growing phenomenon of citizens' journalism through social media has been a great value in providing the first-hand account of Syrian crisis events as they occur in the forms of images, video and audio messages, and information, thus contributing to the enhancement of the general public' situational awareness at real-time. The participants continually negotiate and direct the tension between the negative and positive contradictions to determine the continuity of participation value in social media crowdsourcing.

B. The contradictions of Social Media Crowdsourcing

1. Perceived Usefulness Versus Perceived Risks

In the past few years, the initial role of social computing as a tool to keep in touch with friends, family and colleagues has evolved and become more important mean of communication during emergencies, disasters, and crises [14]. Social media crowdsourcing provides an online environment to communicate, track, and share factual information and hard facts in real time to avoid keeping the crowd in the dark [3] [5] [14]. Furthermore, it provides the people with the opportunity to engage actively in the crises management rather than being merely passive information consumers [5][14].

In Syrian civil war, civilians are employing social media in disseminating, analyzing and sharing information and advices about the sources and places of foods, drinkable water, fuel, emergency medical services and necessary medications. In such societies, social media also represents a valuable channel to send an early warnings raising awareness of the risks and how to respond and act in emergency situations.

As tempting as the capabilities of social media might appear, the incorporation of these new media into the repertoire of crisis management comes with risks that are cannot be neglected. In general, when dealing with any form of outsourcing of tasks, including crowdsourcing, the risks are non-trivial especially for groups that are more distant geographically, culturally, and intellectually where many situations arise that cannot be foresee [21][22]. According to Buecheler et al. [10], with no pre-defined contracts between parties like in traditional outsourcing, crowdsourcing is an extreme case of dealing with the unknown, where the individuals of the crowd are a priori unknown. In essence, by engaging in social media crowdsourcing, the people decide to deal with various degrees of risk of the free actions of others. A number of researchers (e.g., [16][19]) agreed that because of the perceived risks of social media use, users may change their evaluation of membership value over time.

In the periods of political unrest or civil wars, the personal information could lead to activities being left in a vulnerable situation that jeopardizes their wellbeing [5][23]. Protecting activists is one of the most important challenges social media crowdsourcing faces in such societies, particularly in view of the surveillance techniques used by conflict parties to identify the online opponents [5]. Photos, video footage, message or status updates may contain a visual evidence of an individual being present and help identify his identity and disclosing of private and confidential personal details [23]. In such circumstances, activists social media crowdsourcing are encountering a wide range of risks and threats, including, but not limited to, exposing the private information, identity theft, detention or imprisonment, harassment, threats to relatives, torture, kidnapping, or even killing. In many instances, the use of social media by members of the crowds can result in harm to specific individuals who were erroneously identified through vigilante justice and potential harm to responders, including members of the crowd, who may be operating in a crisis [23].

2. Call for Peace versus Incitement to Violence

In war-torn countries, striving to live in peace is a multidimensional motivation that can be fit as a title to the needs for survival and safety. A review of pages, blogs, videos, and posts reveals a third active crowd involved in the current crises striving to end the war. These neutral groups are working hardly to provide reliable information about events of crisis. They are promoting peaceful coexistence, forgiveness, reconciliation, and rejection of foreign interferences. They look for all parties in the conflict in a kindly and conciliatory manner. Sometimes they attack all the parties holding them the responsibility for the killing, destruction, and the displacement of millions of civilians.

Social media crowdsourcing has provided an open arena to these groups to deliver messages about disarmament, peace building, and reconciliation [3][5]. They have a permanent online presence, through their posts, comments, and likes on the online pages and blogs of the parties to the conflict or what so called loyalists and opponents. Furthermore, social media crowdsourcing has allowed the voices of ordinary citizens to be amplified communicating and submitting human rights abuses and committed war crimes. In the Syrian crisis, it has played an influencing role in exposing the use of banned weapons, calling to neutralize civilians and populated residential areas, and maintaining ancient relics. Unfortunately, the voice, activity, and number of these groups are less than those who call for violence taking side to one party of the conflict.

The promotion of violence is a common trend in civil armed conflicts. The growing tension online is going parallel with cases of actual violence [24]. Many previous studies [24][25][26] affirmed the role of social media in catalyzing and amplifying violence by one group against another. Unfortunately, social media became a platform for organized hate groups to recruit, steering, and organize attacks against their antagonists. For example, in the current Syrian civil war, the conflict parties are using social media to incite violence that is fueled by deeply rooted hostility between different ethnic, religious, ideological groups or other minority communities. Antagonists have also used social media to explain how their opponents were planning actions to attack and evict individuals and communities in order to justify the social chaos and vigilante violence against a particular political, ethnic or religious group or any antagonist.

The promotion of extremist rhetoric encouraging violent acts is also a common theme across the terrorist social media platforms [25][26]. Social media crowdsourcing has provided a unique opportunity to disseminate the terrorist ideology and broadcast its messages around the world under cover of religion. Terrorist organizations have increasingly turned to the social media to advocate the incitement to violence using variety of messages promoting and glorifying acts of terrorism, such as suicide attacks.

3. Wisdom versus impulsiveness

The wisdom of crowd is probably one of the first ideas that come to mind when referring to crowdsourcing. In the age of social media, crowdsourcing can be seen as online collective problem solving and a synergy of skills and resources to share wisdom to achieve collective objectives [27][28]. The power of crowdsourcing and harvesting the wisdom of the crowd stand on the collective collaboration through the ability of a group to find better solutions to the same problems, solve more problems than its individual members, and engage in intellectual collaboration in order to create, innovate, and invent [8][27][28]. The most recent studies of crisis management [3][5] reveal that social media supports the creation of informal users' networks facilitating the flow of ideas, and have an important role in the collective generation, dissemination, sharing, and refining of knowledge to assess and response to emergencies.

The outcome of wisdom of the crowd depends to a great extent on the level of coordination and collaborative efforts of crowd members participating in crisis management [5][8]. According to Bellomo et al. [29], unanticipated and unintended irregular motion of individuals into different directions due to strong and rapidly changing forces in crowds lead to the collective confusion and chaos raising the challenge of crowd impulsiveness. Actually, a major challenge that crisis management faces with social media crowdsourcing is the multiplicity and heterogeneity of players and channels of communication that exist during a crisis situation. In this regard, Buecheler et al. [10] demonstrated the risk involved when using crowdsourcing for decision making and to what extent the assumption about the wisdom of the decisions of crowd agents is justified. Roman [15] also explained the inherent weakness of crowdsourcing differentiating between the wisdom of crowds and the "mob that rules" in terms of accuracy, verity, correctness, and the reliability of exchanged information. Polarization between the perceptions of various conflicting crowds is a key issue [3]. Too much data within little time might also trigger fear and anxiety and eventually result in mass panic [7]. According to Kotsiopoulos [30] activists, respondents and security officers may be put at risk by citizens inadvertently exposing sensitive information. The data being inputted by individuals can include moving and still images, location information, temporal information descriptions of needs as well as other information [7]. As a result, existing data sets become quickly outdated and do not reflect people's experience of their current environment.

4. Truth versus rumors

The content of the social media can be the primary source for knowing better and understanding more accurately what is really happening [3][5][14]. The growing phenomenon of citizens' journalism has been a great value in providing the first-hand account of events as they occur in the forms of images, video and audio messages. Many of previous studies (e.g., [1][2]) show that information obtained through crowdsourcing is often more detailed and just as accurate as the information gathered through official channels.

When civilians are faced with uncertainty and lacking a full knowledge of risks, they will look to trusted sources of information for guidance [12]. Actually, the literature reveals widely divergent and mixed views in addressing the truth issues raised by the use of social media in crises. Many of authors (e.g., [3][5][12]) have perceived social media to be more trustworthy than traditional or formal media channels during emergencies and crisis. At the same time there is an apparently contradictory trend (e.g., [23][31]), which believes that the absence of a thorough ethical, legal, and verification framework contributes to the general skepticism towards the trustworthiness of social media in crisis situations. However, the aforementioned views have expressed their concerns, with varying degrees about the trustworthiness of information provided through social media, reliability and credibility of digital volunteers, responsibility and accountability of ICT providers, and the use of misinformation as a weapon of psychological warfare waged by opponents against each other.

War-torn societies live in a world in which vast amount of data are created and stemming from various sources through social media on a constant and ongoing basis. The content of social media does not follow a process of validation to confirm its truthfulness. This abnormal big crisis data represents an area of concern constituting a major challenge against the trustworthiness and competence of such data. For example, rumors, deceptive information, lies, half-truths and facts, myths, counterfeit and fake videos and statements that are spreading on social media became essential elements in the narration of the events in the Syrian civil conflict. Reposting and sharing can make the rumors spread very quickly and get out of control. This could lead to panic in a crowd, which would not be justified by facts but only spread through misinformation [3]. Incidents in Syria crisis showed that crowds have utilized social media to take law enforcement into their own hands based on false information suggesting that certain individuals as being perpetrators [30]. Furthermore, when reporting about a crisis event, people can use different slangs and choose a hashtag or topic they find relevant, making it very difficult to understand the actual content of a post [2]. This results in redundancy of information on different social media tools holding the risk of conflicting facts [31].

5. Sense of Community versus narcissism

The sense of community concept refers to the individuals' subjective feeling of attachment and belongingness to a bigger and stable structure, which can be relied upon for a variety of purposes [32]. People with a strong sense of belonging to a community feel a strong emotional connection to the rest of the members, who support each other and believe that the community can fill their needs and indeed does so. The literature [26][32][33] revealed that the interactive nature of social media helps build a sense of community among individuals from different geographical locations and backgrounds, encouraging the creation of networks to share their feelings, thoughts, and assist each other. Social media and more specifically, SNSs have provided an unprecedented opportunity to bring individuals and groups of people together constituting a new kind of societies seeing beyond the self. According to Subba and Bui [33], the rise of SNSs is resulting in a greater sense of participation, less dependence on official expertise, and a greater trust in collaborative problem solving.

In war-torn societies, SNSs can help create a sense of community that gives individuals the feeling that they are not alone in the crisis and that there are others experiencing similar hardships and difficulties [14]. They have provided a fertile ground for sympathy and empathy sharing the pain of victims. Howell and Taylor [34] explained that what became apparent during crises events is the outpouring of support within and outside communities, and while there was a range of reasons for people starting up community pages and getting involved in social media, the overwhelming driver was a sense of community.

Social media has revealed an entirely new method of self-presentation. A major characteristic of social media is that anyone can create a platform to voice his thoughts and set up his own online participations. The social media represents a source of individual appearance and record the self at the scene of a crisis [23]. Many studies have examined the effects of social media on the increased levels of narcissism [35][36][38]. Narcissism is a pervasive pattern of grandiosity, need for admiration, and an exaggerated sense of self-importance [38]. It is associated with positive self-views traits, including intelligence, physical attractiveness, and power to create a positive impression. The narcissist, rather than experiencing inner growth, is on a path of obsessive focus on self, which acts as a barrier to positive relationships with others. However, social media allows people in crises situations to employ social relationships in order to regulate narcissistic esteem. According to Simsek [37], they can even have more than one identity to present themselves as a complete individual. Narcissists do not focus on interpersonal intimacy, warmth, or other positive aspects of relational outcomes. Instead, they use relationships to appear popular and successful [35]. Posting of selfies on social media is an major trait of narcissism [37].

In civil war, the need of narcissists for sensational coverage of events may create ethical problems when citizen journalists quickly assign blame under weak supporting evidence and exploit the vulnerability of the victims without respect for their opinions, privacy or emotions. Another example is taking selfies in front of victims' bodies to the people killed in the war.

B. Ethical and Technical Solutions

The contradictions of social media crowdsourcing in war-torn societies are showing that the most prevalent challenges revolve around ethical infringements and technical lacunas that have to be addressed. Therefore, the present research suggests ethical and technical solutions to maximize the participation value of social media crowdsourcing in crisis management.

1. Ethical solutions

Social media crowdsourcing is still an evolving field and many of the ethical issues it raises have yet to be resolved. As an increasing number of crowds members involved in crisis management of war-torn societies come to the realization, understanding how to use social media crowdsourcing in an ethically responsible manner is essential to minimize the contradictions of social media crowdsourcing [7]. In war-torn societies, social media crowdsourcing is tightly connected to the off-line society. It not only facilitates the integration of the offline and online environments, but also fosters on-the-ground activities. A malicious member could easily trick crowds to participate in unethical activities online and off-line [2].

The development of appropriate ethical policy can help manage the dilemma between the opportunities and risks of social media crowdsourcing in crises of war-torn societies. In this regard, these communities can leverage the collective knowledge of their members in the form of the ethical principles that define a set of universal principles for humanitarian action. It is important that the providers of social media tools and the digital humanitarian communities emphasize ethical humanitarian service based on a set of ethical rules, standards, codes, values, and philosophy to be followed by the crowds and their members. The ethical policy need to be formulated under the following principles:

- Support the investigation of truthfulness that complies with facts and reality.
- The devised policy must include prescriptive steps to inform and alert the participants in crowdsourcing efforts to behave ethically and avoid dragging behind malevolent actors and crisis profiteers.
- The humanitarian imperative comes first. The protection and neutralization of civilians and populated residential areas, and maintaining ancient relics must be apriority.
- Principles must mandate that data on internally displaced people be given special protections and safeguard their anonymity or privacy. The protection of crowdsourcing participants necessitates hiding any visual evidence of an individual being present and help identify his identity.
- Provide a democratic environment for citizens to participate in the efforts of such crises in terms of freedom to speak, hold opinions, express ideas, discussion, and consensus in which all participants are considered and treated equally.
- The online crowds must provide vulnerable people with assistance without discrimination as to geographic, racial, gender, ethnic, religious beliefs, class or political opinions.
- The crowds must prevent the hate speech, which attacks persons or groups on the basis of certain attributes, such as ethnic origin, religion, gender, race, disability, or political orientation.

2. Technical Solutions

The current civil wars prove that the operators of social media services share the citizens of such societies the challenges of maximizing the value of social media crowdsourcing through minimizing contradictions in the practices of crowds. The present research suggests the following technical solutions to achieve this objective:

- The providers of social medial tools and more specifically SNSs, such as Facebook can add new type of pages or groups that are designed to support the crowdsourcing efforts in crises management.
- As a rule, the user profile data should be protected by design and the sensitive data should never be shared with third parties, nor even be accessible to operators.
- The providers can develop crowd sensing applications based on geospatial crowd sensing to collect data about specific events at particular locations or with dynamic and uncertain participant locations.
- Provide citizens with the best practices, instructions, and guidances to deal with emergencies, evacuation, relieve, and rescue in forms of video, texts or images.
- Provide large scale maps showing the safe places and roads, evacuation routes and conflict hot spots.
- Providing new filtering tools to detect and prevent using any images or video from old or unrelated events.
- Develop new collections of symbols to distinguish between the different kinds of events. Such symbols can help in reducing the redundancy of information making it easier and faster to access specific content that cover a specific event. These symbols are designed to represent, for example, distress calls, calls for blood donation, location of field hospitals, evacuation routes and conflict hot spots.
- Develop new functions to evaluate the reliability and credibility helping users know better which pages, groups, blogs, and digital volunteers can be trusted to become the source of reference. For example, the output of evaluations can be displayed in the form of gradient colors, ranging from green for highly trusted to red for highly untrusted.

IV. CONCLUSION AND FUTURE WORK

Recent emergencies and crises have shown the positive impact of using social media in the collective crises management. Events of the current civil wars in the Middle East are showing a new kind of powerful crisis community, which is made possible by new social media that supports crowdsourcing approaches. The antagonism and differences between and within the crowds become problematic when social media crowdsourcing is used for crisis management purposes in war-torn societies.

Crises arising out of civil wars are very complex, bringing contradictory practices and discursive contexts [6]. Resolving these contradictions becomes the challenge of crisis management stakeholders. Such contradictions embedded in the social media might harm crisis management efforts threatening the life and safety of people. Therefore, the present research aimed to investigate the contradictions and their impact on participation value of social media crowdsourcing in crisis management in war-torn societies incorporating five intrinsic paradoxes. The research presents technical and ethical solutions to enhance the participation value of social media crowdsourcing in crisis management.

The investigation of these contradictions provides a conceptual map, which aims to make sense of the ambiguities and contradictions inherent in social media crowds in war-torn societies. The development of appropriate ethical policy can help manage the dilemma between the opportunities and risks of social media crowdsourcing in crises of war-torn societies. Such communities can leverage the collective knowledge of their members in the form of the ethical principles that define a set of universal principles for humanitarian action based on international humanitarian law. The current civil wars prove that the operators of social media services share the citizens of such societies the challenges of maximizing the value of social media crowdsourcing through minimizing contradictions in the practices of crowds. The present research suggests new type of pages or groups that are designed to support the crowdsourcing efforts and crowds participation in crises management.

There are some limitations, which can serve as directions for future research. The research model needs to be developed and tested empirically. Measurement items can be formulated in terms of motivations and threats or positive and negative practices. Data can be collected from Syrian refugees or the Syrian society itself using an online survey. There are thousands of pages and groups on social networking sites, created by Syrian activists, dedicated to Syrian crisis issues. These platforms can be employed effectively to distribute the online survey. Furthermore, the future research needs to investigate the factors affecting the appearance of these online contradictions. The future research also has to discuss in more details how each solution will address the contradictions. Finally, the suggested technical solutions need further technical validation and intensive research in order to evaluate their applicability.

REFERENCES

[1] J. Peng, Z. Yanmin, S. Wei, and W. Min-You, "When data contributors meet multiple crowdsourcers: Bilateral competition in mobile crowdsourcing," Computer Networks, 95, 2016, pp. 1-14.

[2] G. Schimak, H. Denis, and P. Jasmin, "Crowdsourcing in crisis and disaster management–challenges and considerations," In International Symposium on Environmental Software Systems, 2015, pp. 56-70. Springer International Publishing, 2015.

[3] C. Wendling, R. Jack, and J. Stephane , "The use of social media in risk and crisis communication," 24. OECD Publishing, Paris, 2013.

[4] J. Rogstadius, V. Maja, C. Teixeira, K. Vassilis, and A. Jim Alain, "CrisisTracker: Crowdsourced social media curation for disaster awareness," IBM Journal of Research and Development, 57(5), 2013, pp. 4-1.

[5] L. Sweta, "Early warning systems and disaster management using mobile crowdsourcing," International Journal of Science and Research, 3(4), 2014, pp. 356-365.

[6] A. Lambert, "Disaster Data Assemblages: Five Perspectives on Social Media and Communities in Response and Recovery," ," Proc. The System Sciences (HICSS), 2016 49th Hawaii International Conference on, pp. 2237-2245. IEEE, 2016.

[7] R. Finn, W. Hayley, and W. Kush, "Exploring big 'crisis' data in action: potential positive and negative externalities," Proc. ISCRAM 2015 Conference, Kristiansand, Norway. 2015, pp. 1-6.

[8] J. Howe, "The rise of crowdsourcing," Wired magazine, 14(6), 2006, pp. 1-4.

[9] C. Chiu, T. Liang, and E. Turban, "What can crowdsourcing do for decision support? Decision Support Systems," 65, 2014, pp. 40-49.

[10] T. Buecheler, J. Sieg, R. Füchslin, and R. Pfeifer, "Crowdsourcing, Open Innovation and Collective Intelligence in the Scientific Method-A Research Agenda and Operational Framework,", In ALIFE, 2010, pp. 679-686.

[11] D. Brabham, "The myth of amateur crowds: A critical discourse analysis of crowdsourcing coverage," Information, Communication & Society,15(3), 2012, pp. 394-410.

[12] A. Jain, et al., "Mobile Application Development for Crisis Data," Procedia Engineering, 107, 2015, pp.255-262.

[13] J. Qadir, et al., "Crisis analytics: big data-driven crisis response," Journal of International Humanitarian Action, 1(1), pp.1-8.

[14] N. Kaufmann, T. Schulze, and D. Veit, D., "More than fun and money. Worker Motivation in Crowdsourcing-A Study on Mechanical Turk,". In *AMCIS*, Vol. 11, pp. 1-11.

[15] J. Goncalves, et al., "Crowdsourcing on the spot: altruistic use of public displays, feasibility, performance, and behaviours," *Proc.* ACM international joint conference on Pervasive and ubiquitous computing (pp. 753-762). ACM.

[16] C. Annamalai, S. Koay, and S. Lee, "Role of Social Networking in Disaster Management: An Empirical Analysis," Journal of Computation in Biosciences and Engineering, 1(3), 2014, pp. 1-5.

[17] C. Huang, E. Chan, and A. Hyder, " Web 2.0 and internet social networking: A new tool for disaster management?-lessons from Taiwan," BMC medical informatics and decision making, 10(1), (2010), pp. 57-69.

[18] D. Yates and S. Paquette, " Emergency knowledge management and social media technologies: A case study of the 2010 Haitian earthquake," International journal of information management, 31(1), 2011, pp. 6-13.

[19] D. Roman, "Crowdsourcing and the question of expertise," Communications of the ACM, 52(12), 2009, pp. 12-12.

[20] B. Debatin, J. Lovejoy, A. Horn, and B. Hughes, "Facebook and online privacy: Attitudes, behaviors, and unintended consequences," Journal of Computer-Mediated Communication, 15(1), 2009,pp. 83-108.

[21] F. Stutzman, R. Capra, and J. Thompson, "Factors mediating disclosure in social network sites," Computers in Human Behavior, 27(1), 2010, pp. 590-598.

[22] H. Watson, L. Baruh, R. Finn, and S. Scifo, "Citizen (in) security?: social media, citizen journalism and crisis response," Proc. The 11th International Conference on Information Systems for Crisis Response and Management (ISCRAM). May 2014, pp. 399-303.

[23] I. Gagliardone, D. Gal, T. Alves, and G. Martinez, "Countering Online Hate Speech," UNESCO, France.

[24] M. Ally and M. Gardiner, "The moderating influence of device characteristics and usage on user acceptance of Smart Mobile Devices," Proc. The 23rd Australasian Conference on Information Systems, 2012, pp. 1-10, ACIS.

[25] United Nations Office on Drugs and Crimes, "The Use of the Internet for Terrorist Purposes," United Nations, New York, 2012, https://www.unodc.org/documents/frontpage/Use_of_Internet_for_Terrorist_Purposes.pdf, 2012, pp. 1–158, [retrieved: March, 2017].

[26] M. Martinez and W. Bryn, "The wisdom of crowds: The potential of online communities as a tool for data analysis," Technovation, 34(4), 2014, pp. 203-214.

[27] P. Lévy, "From social computing to reflexive collective intelligence: The IEML research program," Information Sciences, 180(1), 2010, pp. 71-94.

[28] N. Bellomo, L. Clarke, P. Gibelli, P. Townsend, and B. Vreugdenhil, "Human behaviours in evacuation crowd dynamics: from modelling to "big data" toward crisis management," Physics of life reviews, 18(1), 2016, pp. 1-21.

[29] I. Kotsiopoulos, "Social Media in Crisis Management: Role, Potential, and Risk," Proc. In Utility and Cloud Computing (UCC), IEEE/ACM 7th International Conference on, 2014, December, pp. 681-686, IEEE.

[30] S. Mukherjee "The Use of Twitter, Facebook, LinkedIn etc. as Strategic Tools for Crisis Communication," International Journal of Management and International Business Studies, 4(2), 2014, pp. 175-180.

[31] A. Lev-On, "Communication, community, crisis: Mapping uses and gratifications in the contemporary media environment," New Media Society, 14(1), 2011, pp. 98-116.

[32] R. Subba and T., Bui, "An Exploration of Physical-Virtual Convergence Behaviors in Crisis Situations," Proc. In System Sciences (HICSS), 2010 43rd Hawaii International Conference, 2010, January, pp. 1-10, IEEE.

[33] M. Taylor, G. Wells, G. Howell, and B. Raphael, "The role of social media as psychological first aid as a support to community resilience building," Australian Journal of Emergency Management, 27(1), 2012, pp. 20-26.

[34] S. Mehdizadeh, "Self-presentation 2.0: Narcissism and self-esteem on Facebook," Cyberpsychology, behavior, and social networking, 13(4), 2010, pp. 357-364.

[35] E. Ong, et al., "Narcissism, extraversion and adolescents' self-presentation on Facebook," Personality and individual differences, 50(2), 2011, pp. 180-185.

[36] T. Ryan and X., "Who uses Facebook? An investigation into the relationship between the Big Five, shyness, narcissism, loneliness, and Facebook usage," Computers in Human Behavior, 27(5), 2011, pp. 1658-1664.

[37] A. Simsek, "Techno-psychological Aspects of Social Media Behaviors," Journalism and Mass Communication, 5(6), 2015, pp. 270-278.

[38] J. Fox and C. Margaret, "The Dark Triad and trait self-objectification as predictors of men's use and self-presentation behaviors on social networking sites, " Personality and Individual Differences, 76(1), 2015, pp. 161-165.

AGILE Web Development using WebBPMN

Riccardo Cognini
Research Unit
e-Linking Online System
Camerino (MC), Italy
Email: riccardo.cognini@e-lios.eu

Alberto Polzonetti
Research Unit
e-Linking Online System
Camerino (MC), Italy
Email: alberto.polzonetti@e-lios.eu

***Abstract*—In recent years, many web applications regulated by workflows were developerd in order to permit the collaboration between many stakeholders during the execution of Business Processes. Generally, these kind of systems are implemented using web technologies in order to be easily designed, implemented and to be available in different operative systems and platform. Standard general purpose Business Process Modeling languages such as BPMN (Business Process Modeling and Notation) can be used to design the workflow of these systems, but they lack in the definition of which web technology has to be used to implement each single business activity. Another problem due to the complexity of this application is to choose the right software design process to be flexible enought to deal with changes in requirements and in software code itself. In this paper, we propose a novel business process modeling notation named webBPMN including elements that can be used to model web applications regulated by workflows. The notation can be combined with AGILE design process in order to develop flexible web application. We experimented the approach designing the Business Process of the internship web application of the University of Camerino.**

Keywords–Web Application; Business Process; Metamodel.

I. INTRODUCTION

Inter-organizational Business Processes (BPs) permit to different stakeholders to successfully cooperate in order to reach a common target goal [1]. Each stakeholder involved in the BP pursues its objectives within the cooperation and shares its competencies and processes to provide the integrated functionality. Implementing a software system that allows that cooperation among different stakeholders is not an easy task. It requires a deep analysis of requirements, activities flow and how the actors interact.

Furthermore, many software systems are web based applications in which there are many stakeholders that collaborate in the same environment [2]. In several cases, these software systems are based on a BP, it means that stakeholders have to perform in a specific way a predefined set of activities in order to reach goals. For instance, in an e-commerce web site there is a specific BP that drive the buyer and the seller in order to complete the purchasing of goods.

One of the main issues during the design phase of a software system is the definition of the flow of activities that have to be performed by stakeholders [3]. Languages such as Business Process Modeling and Notation (BPMN) [4], UML Activity Diagram (UML AD) [5], Yet Another Workflow Language (YAWL) [6] or EPC [7] are used to define the flow of activities in imperative way. The main problem of these languages is that they are general purpose and do not provide specific elements to design workflows for web based applications.

Another issues in software engineering is to find a suitable way to reach all the requirements and the request of customers. Traditional software engineering design processes such as waterfall or iterative approaches lack in flexibility since they are to structured and they do not react to requirement chenges.

In this paper, we propose webBPMN, a BPMN 2.0 variation, in order to include elements that can be used to design web application based on BP using an AGILE development technique. In particular, we consider new types of tasks and sub-processes assuming that a single atomic activity can be performed in single *Web Page Task* and that a web page can be used in order to perform many activities, then it is a *Web Page Sub-Process*. Other elements to specify client/server side functions and events are also designed. We also comabine webBPMN with the AGILE process in order to design a software that implement a structured procedure but at the same time it is quick and reactive to changes.

The proposed approach was used to design the BP of the internship procedure of the University of Camerino. Its software system was implemented starting from a webBPMN model.

The paper is structured as follow. Section II provides background material related to BP modeling and AGILE. In Section III the webBPMN notation is explained, the in Section IV the approach is described. Then Section V is about related works and, finally, in Section VI we treat some conclusions.

II. BACKGROUND

In this section background materials about Business Process Management and AGILE are provided.

A. *Business Process Management*

Business Process Management (BPM) "includes concepts, methods, and techniques to support the design, administration, configuration, enactment, and analysis of Business Processes" [8]. "A BP is a collection of related and structured activities undertaken by one or more organizations in order to pursue some particular goal. Within an organization a BP results in the provisioning of services or in the production of goods for internal or external stakeholders" [9]. Public services structure, their input and output, the interdependencies among different elements can be modeled and implemented using notations and tools supporting the BP abstraction.

The accuracy of the BP modeling phase is critical for the success of an organization in particular in scenarios in

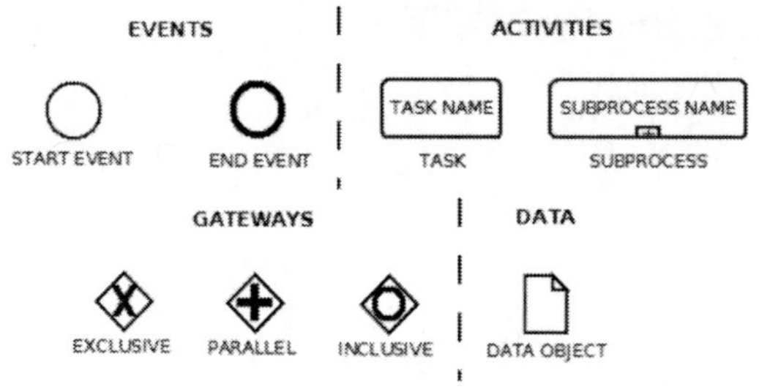

Figure 1. BPMN 2.0 Core Elements.

which it is necessary to adapt to changing requirements. In order to design a BP different classes of languages have been investigated and defined.

In our work, we refer to BPMN 2.0 an Object Management Group standard [4]. It is the most used language by domain experts due to its intuitive graphical notation. We have mainly used process diagrams, focusing on the point of view of system users. The following BPMN 2.0 elements (Figure 1) are the core elements of the language and those we will use on the approach.

- **Events**, which are used to represent something that can happen. An Event can be *Start Event* represents the points in which the BP starts, and *End Event* is raised when the BP terminates. Events are drawn as circles.
- **Activities**, which are used to represent a generic work that a company performs within a BP. An Activity can be atomic - *Task* - or not - *Sub-Process*. Activities are drawn as rectangles with rounded corners.
- **Gateways**, which are used to manage the flow of BP both for parallel activities and choices. Different types of gateways are available, the most used are followed reported. *Parallel Gateway* has to wait all their input flows to start and then all the output paths are started in parallel, it can behave as a fork respects to output paths or as a merge respects to input paths. *Exclusive Gateway* gives the possibility to describe choices both in input and output, it can be activated each time the gateway is reached and when executed it can activate exactly one output path. *Inclusive Gateway* gives the possibility to select among multiple output paths each time they are reached, it can behave also as inclusive merge. Gateways are drawn as diamonds.
- **Data Objects**, which permit to model documents, data, and other objects used and updated during the BP. Objects can also be characterized by a state. An activity can require or can generate a data object in a particular state, whereas if the state is not explicitly reported the activity is state independent. A data object cannot be in two different states at the same time. If the same object is linked to the same activity specifying two different states, this means that states are exclusive with respect to each other, therefore when the activity is executed it needs the data object in one of the available states. A Data Object is represented by a portrait-oriented rectangle that has its upper-right corner folded over. States are represented using text within squared brackets located under the object name.

Using BPMN it is also possible to define the participants (or stakeholders) involved in a BP. *Pools* can be used as elements containers in order to specify the activities that have to be executed by a single participant, they are represented via rectangle containers. Participants can communicate each other using *Message Flow* that specify that a particular task or event can be performed only if a message from another participant is received. *Message Flow* are graphically represented via a dotted arrows. An example of BPMN model in which participants communicates is shown in Figure 2. The BP shows that there are two participants, they are *Participant 1* and *Participant 2*. *Participant 1* starts the execution of the BP and then he sends a message to *Participant 2* executing the task *Send a Message*. *Participant 2* starts the execution of his BP when he receives the message from *Participant 1*, it is why there is a *Start Message Event*. Then, *Participant 2* executes the tasks *Check the Message* and *Responde* in order to send a message to *Participant 1* and ending his BP. When *Participant 1* receives this message, he has to choose if execute the task *Do Action 1* or *Do Action 2*. After the execution of the chosen task the BP execution ends.

B. Agile Web Development

An agile approach to web development is an attitude that promotes adaptation, cross-functionality, and continual collaboration amongst a team. To be agile, programmers and Project Manager must constantly be thinking months in advance and must adapt to any changes that may happen. They are planning early on, meeting with your team in scrum huddles, establishing deliverables, meeting goals ahead of schedule and making continual improvements. It is necessary that the team is completely flexible to changes during the development process. Within this flexibility, the team anticipates changes and respond accordingly, then the team must predict, execute and adapt.

A cornerstone of agile web development is also the scrum process in which the team has a quick meeting, discusses progress and implementation, and then goes their separate ways, while still functioning as an autonomous unit. Afterward, all relevant information is continually relayed to the client and the projects are divided into sprints and user stories. It helps foster proper communication and maintain an ideal agency/client relationship. Adopting an agile process helps eliminate unnecessary wastes of time and allows software companies to allocate those precious minutes and hours on actions and processes that add value to your website. Agile web development can easily be summed up with one word: efficiency. Compared to traditional software engineering, agile software development mainly targets complex systems and product development with dynamic, non-deterministic and non-linear characteristics, where accurate estimates, stable plans, and predictions are often hard to get in early stagesand big up-front designs and arrangements would probably cause a lot of waste, i.e., are not economically sound. These basic arguments and previous industry experiences, learned from years of successes and failures, iterative and evolutionary development [10].

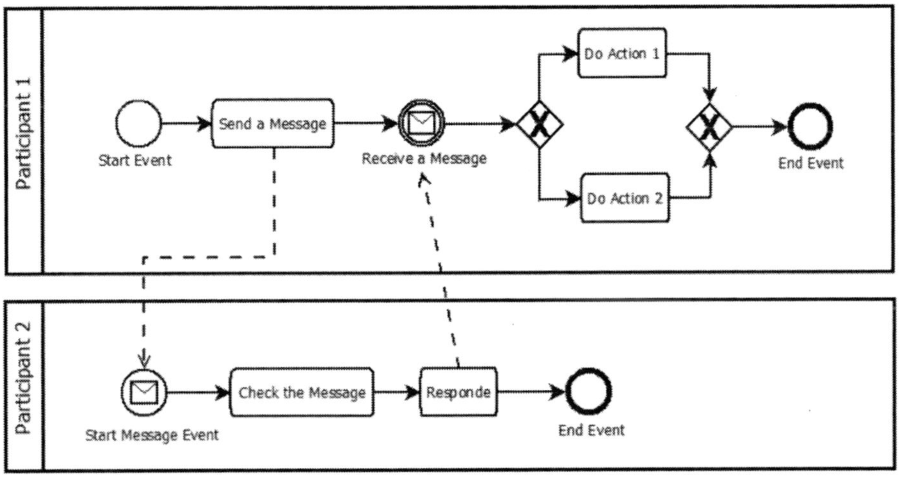

Figure 2. BPMN 2.0 Model Example.

C. The SCRUM Approach

Scrum appraoch is written from the perspective of the customer. By thinking of what the customer desires/needs, it allows the development team to better understand how to achieve goals for the website. A simple way to look at this is to think of this by using the following sentence: As a (role) I want (feature) so that (benefits). As you collect user stories, you begin to acquire a product backlog, which is a collection of user stories. These helps facilitate direction and milestones. There are three core roles in the Scrum framework. These core roles are ideally collocated to deliver potentially shippable Product Increments. They represent the Scrum Team. Although other roles involved with product development may be encountered, Scrum does not define any team roles other than those described below.

- **Product Ownner** The Product Owner represents the product's stakeholders and the voice of the customer; and is accountable for ensuring that the team delivers value to the business. The Product Owner writes customer-centric items (typically user stories), prioritizes them based on importance and dependencies, and adds them to the Product Backlog. Scrum Teams should have one Product Owner [11].
- **Development Team** The Development Team is responsible for delivering potentially shippable increments (PSIs) of product at the end of each Sprint (the Sprint goal). A team is made up of 39 individuals who do the actual work (analyse, design, develop, test, technical communication, document, etc.). Development Teams are cross-functional, with all the skills as a team necessary to create a Product Increment. The Development Team in Scrum is self-organizing, even though there may be some interaction with a project management office.
- **Scrum Master** Scrum is facilitated by a Scrum Master, who is accountable for removing impediments to the ability of the team to deliver the product goals and deliverables. The Scrum Master is not a traditional team lead or project manager, but acts as a buffer between the team and any distracting influences. The Scrum Master ensures that the Scrum framework is followed. The Scrum Master helps to ensure the team follows the agreed processes in the Scrum framework, often facilitates key sessions, and encourages the team to improve. The role has also been referred to as a team facilitator or servant-leader to reinforce these dual perspectives [12]

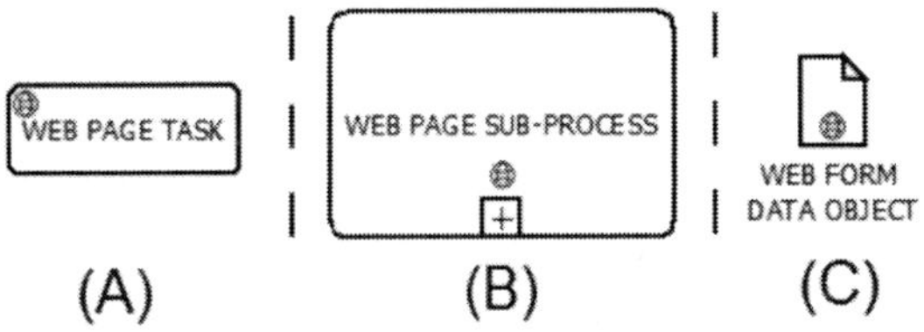

Figure 3. webBPMN Main Elements.

III. WebBPMN

The proposed language named webBPMN is a BPMN 2.0 variation in which standard BPMN tasks and sub-processes are replaced with activities designed for web based applications implementing workflows. A new type of data object is also introduced in order to model the type of data used by web pages to communicate. These kinds of elements are described as follow.

- **Web Page Task** is an atomic activity performed in a generic single web page (Figure 3-A). When the activity is performed a new page will be open. In this kind of task the stakeholder has to interact with the software system via a web page. For instance, a *Web Page Task* can be related to a search page or a form that the stakeholder has to fill;
- **Web Page Sub-Process** is a composed activity performed in a complex web page (Figure 3-B). In this kind of activity the stakeholder should perform more that one activities in a single page beside client side technologies (such as Javascript/AJAX) or/and some

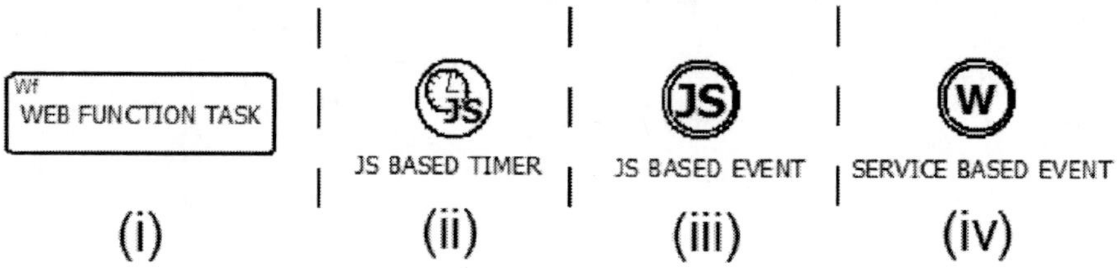

Figure 4. webBPMN Elements that can be used in a Web Page Sub-Process.

events can happen. For instance a *Web Page Sub-Process* can be used to represent a page in which a web chat is implemented. A *Web Page Sub-Process* may contain a set of specific BP elements that are able to specify the behaviours of the activity. Such as in many others BPMN sub-processes a start and and end event should be insert. The list of elements that can be inserted inside are described as follow.

- ◦ **Web Function Task** is an atomic activity that can be performed in a web page without open a new page (Figure 4-i). It can be performed automatically or manually by an user, it can be client or server side. For instance, it can be used to call a web service in asynchronous way or to perform any server side request via AJAX;
- ◦ **JavaScript Based Timer** is an event that is trigged by a timer for 1 or more times (Figure 4-ii). For instance, it can be used to refresh the page or to update the list of messages and users connected in a web chat;
- ◦ **JavaScript Based Event** is a generic client side event that can be trigged by an user action such as change the value in a dropdown list (Figure 4-iii). For instance, it can be used to represent the event that is trigged when there is an error in a Web Form input field. When an event like that is trigged a *Web Function Task* should be performed;
- ◦ **Service Based Event** is a generic event that is trigged when a Web Service respondes to a call (Figure 4-iv). For instance, it can be used to start activities when a login server responds to a request;

- **Web Form Data Object** is a particular type of data that can be generated by a web form (Figure 3-C), it means that it can be generated only by a *Web Page Task* or a *Web Page Sub-Process*. A *Web Form Data Object* is composed by a set of values and eventually by a set of data files. This data object is generated by a web page and it can be consumed by another web page. For instance, this data object can be generated by a form in which an user has to log into the web application and then it can be consumed in another page in order to verify the credentials.

Using webBPMN a BP designer can use all the standard BPMN 2.0 elements except tasks and sub-processes. Pools should be used to define which web pages can be accessible by a specific stakeholders. The interaction between stakeholders can be defined via standard BPMN *Message Flows*. Gateways are used to drive the route of the flow and define which pages should be open for each stakeholder.

IV. The Approach

The approach that we proposed expects three different steps.

- The first step is performed by Software designer with skills in BP modeling. Using a story telling approach, he collects all the requirement by the customers. The requirement will be grouped in order to divide the work in different modules. Each modul can be implemented by one or more programmers. To be Agile in this step, the Software designer should divide the requirements using the SCRUM approach [13]. In this specific context the Software designer can be considered the SCRUM Master.
- In the second step, the Software Designer designer model the webBPMN model of the web application. From this point until the end of the development he will work as SCRUM Master, so he will remove impediments that afflict the development team.
- In the last step, starting from the webBPMN models the development team starts to implement each singol task. After each task implementation there is a meeting with the Product Ownner in order to evaluate the work that was done.

A. Use Case

The described approach has been applied to model the Web Application of the Students Internship Business Process of the University of Camerino. This is a service that the Univeristy has to put in place in order to permit studens to start an internship in Italian Companies - in University of Camerino each Bachelor student must do an internship to graduate. The proposed webBPMN is shown in Figure 5, it is just a simplied version of the real one.

Three stakeholders are involved in this business process, the student that has to apply for an internship, the related company and the Internship office of the University.

The trigger of a process instance is the student that has to do an internship. First, the student accesses to the Login Page that is modeled as a Web Page Sub-Process since several function are needed to verify the identity of the student. The Web Function Task *Request ESSE3 credentias* is delegated to request username and password of the student, then the Web Function Task *Connect to ESSE3 (LDAP Server)* connects the user to ESSE3 system in which credentials are stored. The

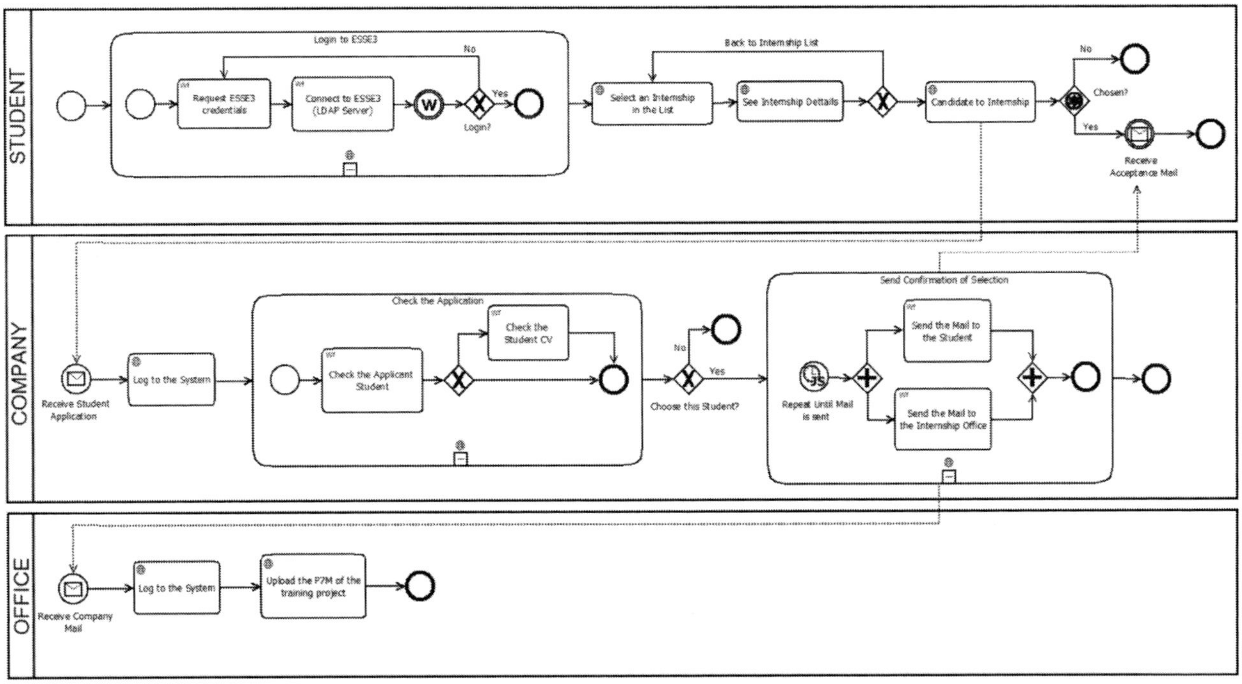

Figure 5. Internship BP of University of Camerino.

response arrives in the Service Based Event, if the credentials are correct the page related to the *Select an Internship in the List* Web Page Task is open. In this page, the student can see the list of available internships, he/she can choose one of them in order to open the detail page of the internship specified by the *See Internship Details* Web Task Page. The student can candidate to the internship or return to the page in which there is the list.

When the student applies for an internship the related company receives a communication. Then, the company will log to the system via the *Log to the System* Web Page Task in order to check the student application in the *Check Application* Web Page Sub-Process. In this page the company checks the information about the student (*Check the Applicant Student* Web Function Task) and, optionally his CV (*Check the Student CV* Web Function Task). The company can choose the student for the internship of not, in case the student is chosen the *Send Confirmation of Selection* Web Page Sub-Process is open. In this page, e-mails are sent to the student and to the Internship office of the University via *Send the Mail to the Student* and *Send the Mail to the Internship Office* Web Function Tasks. These tasks are performed automatically by an JavaScript Based Timer that repeat the execution until mails are sent correctly.

When the company chooses a student for an internship, the Internship office receives a mail. The office has to log to the system via the *Log to the System* Web Page Task and then upload the P7M file related to the internship via the *Upload the P7M of the training project* Web Page Task.

Notwithstanding the complexity of the Web Application modeling of the scenario has revealed that webBPMN permits to define which activities have to be performed in each web page.

V. RELATED WORK

In literature, there are just few languages to model web applications. Usually, languages provide few models to design different requirements of the web the applications.

The model Object Oriented Hypermedia (OO-H) is used to design generic web applications [14]. In particular, OO-H provides a navigation model named Navigation Access Diagram (NAD) that provides the necessary constructs to represent how web site user navigates between links. It is similar to the concept explained in this paper in which web pages are represented as business activities, but the used semantics is not able to represent the activities that can be performed in each web page. There are some language similar to OO-H such as Object-Oriented Hypermedia Design Method (OOHDM) [15], they share the same base approach.

Another interesting language is UML-based Web Engineering (UWE) that is an object oriented and iterative approach based on UML [16]. Also in this language, there is a navigation model to specify how users navigate between links of the web site. Also in this case, the activities that users have to perform in each page are not defined by the model.

Web Modeling Language (WebML) is a language to design web sites [17]. It provides an high-level graphical representation providing different models in order to design several aspects of the designed web application. In this case there is the Composition Model that specifies the pages provided by the web application, instead the Navigation Model specifies how pages are linked together.

The main issue of these language is that they are not focused on the BP modeling. They can be used to design a generic web site also if it is not regulated by a BP. It means that they do not provide a full specification to manage all the possible situations that can happen in a BP. Instead, thanks to BPMN base notation webBPMN provides a set of elements that can be used to describe many situation and, thanks to the variation of the semantics of the BPMN activities it is possible to adapt the language for the web application modeling.

A language similar to webBPMN is WebWorkFlow that is an object oriented workflow modeling language [18]. It can be used to design simple activities flows for web application. The main lack of the language is that it does not provide a graphical representation since it is mainly used to generate an executable application. It means than also the elements provided by the language are not so much and their semantics are more related to programming languages than BPs.

VI. Conclusion and Further Work

In this paper, we present an approach that combine a BP modeling language with AGILE approach in order to design web application in more efficient wway. The BP notation proposed seems particularly suitable to specify which functions have to be implemented in which web page and the AGILE approach seems to be very useful to understand better the requirements and the needs of the customers. The experiment related to University of Camerino Internship BP provides encouraging results.

In the next future we plan to extend the webBPMN notation including new elements in order to specify in a better way web technologies and functions. For instance, we will include the concepts of Session and Cookies extending again the BPMN data objects. We are implementing a modeling environment to use the webBPMN notation, we are using ADOxx (http://adoxx.org/) to design the webBPMN meta-model. At the end, we will continue the experimental work considering other use cases in the e-government scenario.

Acknowledgment

The authors would like to thank the University of Camerino.

References

[1] V. Vathanophas, "Business process approach towards an inter-organizational enterprise system," Business Process Management Journal, vol. 13, no. 3, 2007, pp. 433–450.

[2] A. Ginige and S. Murugesan, "Web engineering: an introduction," MultiMedia, IEEE, vol. 8, no. 1, Jan 2001, pp. 14–18.

[3] M. Dumas, W. M. van der Aalst, and A. H. ter Hofstede, Process-aware Information Systems: Bridging People and Software Through Process Technology. New York, NY, USA: John Wiley & Sons, Inc., 2005.

[4] B. P. M. OMG, "Notation (bpmn) version 2.0 (2011)," Available on: http://www. omg. org/spec/BPMN/2.0, 2011.

[5] OMG, OMG Unified Modeling Language (OMG UML), Superstructure, Version 2.4.1, Object Management Group Std., Rev. 2.4.1, August 2011. [Online]. Available: http://www.omg.org/spec/UML/2.4.1

[6] W. M. Van Der Aalst and A. H. Ter Hofstede, "Yawl: yet another workflow language," Information systems, vol. 30, no. 4, 2005, pp. 245–275.

[7] J. Mendling, "Event-driven process chains (epc)," in Metrics for Process Models, ser. Lecture Notes in Business Information Processing. Springer Berlin Heidelberg, 2008, vol. 6, pp. 17–57. [Online].

[8] M. Weske, Business process management concepts, languages, architectures, 1st ed. Springer, Nov. 2007.

[9] A. Lindsay, D. Downs, and K. Lunn, "Business process - attempts to find a definition," Information and Software Technology, vol. 45, 2003, pp. 1015–1019.

[10] C. Larman, Agile and iterative development: a manager's guide. Addison-Wesley Professional, 2004.

[11] R. Pichler, Agile Product Management with Scrum: Creating Products that Customers Love (Adobe Reader). Addison-Wesley Professional, 2010.

[12] E. Leybourn, Directing the Agile organisation: A lean approach to business management. IT Governance Ltd, 2013.

[13] J. Sutherland and K. Schwaber, "The scrum guide," The Definitive Guide to Scrum: The Rules of the Game. Scrum. org, 2013.

[14] P. Plessers, O. D. Troyer, and S. Casteleyn, "Event-based modeling of evolution for semantic-driven systems," in Advanced Information Systems Engineering, 17th International Conference, CAiSE 2005, Porto, Portugal, June 13-17, 2005, Proceedings, 2005, pp. 63–76. [Online]. Available:

[15] D. Schwabe and G. Rossi, "An object oriented approach to web-based applications design," Theor. Pract. Object Syst., vol. 4, no. 4, Oct. 1998, pp. 207–225. [Online]. Available: http://dx.doi.org/10.1002/(SICI)1096-9942(1998)4:4¡207::AID-TAPO2¿3.0.CO;2-2

[16] N. Koch and A. Kraus, "Towards a common metamodel for the development of web applications," in Web Engineering, ser. Lecture Notes in Computer Science, J. Lovelle, B. Rodrguez, J. Gayo, M. del Puerto Paule Ruiz, and L. Aguilar, Eds. Springer Berlin Heidelberg, 2003, vol. 2722, pp. 497–506. [Online]. Available:

[17] S. Ceri, P. Fraternali, and A. Bongio, "Web modeling language (webml): a modeling language for designing web sites," Computer Networks, vol. 33, no. 1, 2000, pp. 137–157.

[18] Z. Hemel, R. Verhaaf, and E. Visser, "Webworkflow: an object-oriented workflow modeling language for web applications," in Model Driven Engineering Languages and Systems. Springer, 2008, pp. 113–127.

Semiotic Annotation of Video Commercials: Why the artifact is the way it is?

Elio Toppano
Dipartimento di Scienze Matematiche, Informatiche e Fisiche (DIMA)
University of Udine
Via delle Scienze, 208 – Udine (Italy)

Abstract—**Traditionally, semantic annotation of audiovisual texts is used to describe expressive features and content of a product for a more efficient and effective browsing, retrieval, filtering or reuse of the resource. Drawing on semiotic theories, this paper proposes a new concept of annotation – called semiotic annotation – whose goal is to describe the multilayered structure of meanings inscribed within the audiovisual by its author/designer. The advantages of this kind of annotation is discussed with respect to means/ends analysis of video commercials. A case study is then illustrated that exploits a semiotic compliant informal ontology proposed in a previous work to assess the effectiveness of the conceptualization and the annotation method.**

Keywords-video; content annotation; semantic web; semiotics.

I. INTRODUCTION

According to a recent report published by Cisco [1] video is currently representing and will represent in the future - together with gaming - one of most important parts of the global Internet traffic growth. We may expect that video advertising will follow this trend and thus will be a fast-growing opportunity on line and one of the most promising ad formats in the future. Nowadays, web video advertising covers a wide range of products differing in production quality, time length and distribution. The universe of content is broad and varied ranging from professionally produced content, generally, repurposed from Broadcast Video and Cable Networks to clips created and uploaded by everyday people, i.e., user generated content.

Distribution and formats also vary ranging from linear and non-linear in-stream video to in-display video and combinations thereof packaged together in a compelling way [2]. Most ad videos are narratives, that is, they told a micro-story aimed at presenting a product-service or communicating brand identity. This paper is about video annotation [3]. We address this problem following a communication-based design approach [4] according to which video is seen as a *mediator* between the intentions of the designer (i.e., author) and the interpretation of the user.

Intentions (e.g., brand's identity communication, product advertising) are assumed to be inscribed within the artifact through *semantic transformation* [5] and implicitly communicated to the user by the video expression and content. In the following, we will take the perspective of the author/designer of the video rather than the final user. We are interested in how meaning is intentionally constructed and articulated during the design process, how it shapes the audiovisual and how users can infer the designer's intentions – both informative and persuasive - and recognize *that they are users*, i.e., that their experiences with the product have been anticipated. In line with this objective, annotation is conceived of as an activity aimed at describing the *experiential project* envisaged by the author and embodied within the product [6]. It is performed by the author/designer during the development of the audiovisual artifact and requires a set of annotation descriptors (i.e., concepts and relative terminological realizations) that could be used not only to describe how the artifact is made and functions but also why it is the way it is. The paper is organized as follows. The next section elaborates more on the motivations lying behind our work. Section III introduces the concept of *Semiotic Annotation* which is at the core of our approach. Section IV summarizes some basic requirements the design of an ontology supporting the approach should satisfy and suggests a possible solution. Section V describes a method for video annotation and exemplifies it in a specific case. Section VI discusses benefits and limitations of the approach. Finally, Section VII draws some conclusions.

II. MOTIVATIONS

The term *annotation* can be understood in two different ways: i) as an activity (i.e., the process by means of which metadata are attached to other data) and ii) as the result of the activity. [7] proposed a formalization of annotation in terms of a quadruple: the annotated data (i.e., the subject of annotation), the annotating data (i.e., the object of annotation), the annotation relation (i.e., the predicate that defines the type of relationship between annotated and annotating data) and the context in which the annotation is made. Traditionally - see for example Mpeg7 [8] [9] - metadata are used to describe the expressive characteristics (e.g., visual and audio features) or the semantic content of an entire multimedia product or of specific product fragments.

Contextual information, if present, refers to the people involved in the development of the document (e.g., the scriptwriter, the video-maker, the sound designer), the place and time of its production, its spatial and temporal scope, the target user. Seldom if ever, contextual metadata refer to the design process itself, such as, for example the designer's intentions behind the product, the effects that the designer intends to evoke in the user, the rationale behind specific functional and expressive design choices. As a consequence, traditional annotation approaches do not allow means/ends analyses [10]. For example, they do not support neither *teleological explanations* (i.e., Why the artifact is the way it is?) nor *causal explanations* (i.e., How a specific communicative goal/intention or impression has been achieved in terms of specific visual and aural choices and compositions). The rationale is that the aim of current annotation approaches is more focused on product filtering, retrieval and reuse of documents than on critical analysis, explanation and evaluation. Following recent developments in the field of Interaction Criticism [11], and Design for Experience [12] [13] we claim that means/ends metadata could add value to the product and could be useful both for the designers and the users. More specifically, designers could exploit this knowledge:

- for highlighting the concerns and design choices made during multimedia development;
- for the analysis and comparison of multimedia products during the phase of competing analysis in order to understand *why* they are designed the way they are and *how* they differ from one to another;
- for the synthesis of new products because means/ends metadata implicitly codify design knowledge that can be fruitfully extracted and reused in new projects;
- for the evaluation of the internal coherence of products because means/ends metadata explicate the relationships existing between design choices taken at different aggregation and abstraction levels;
- for the "diagnosis and repair" of communication because means/ends metadata allow the identification of symptoms (i.e., discrepancies between the intended meaning of the product and the actual one) and the localization of causes.

These activities are particularly important in some application domains such as transmedia projects, web marketing, brand driving and management where issues related to the differentiation of advertisement products (e.g., web sites, advergames, video clip, etc.), internal product coherence, effective communication of brand identity, time consistency of portfolio products are paramount. The annotation of multimedia product with means/ends metadata could be also useful to the user:

- to make more informed choices, i.e., to better understand if a product is adequate with respect to her values, needs, desires, preferences;
- to better exploit the concept of *genre* in document retrieval. This is because means/ends annotation allows to anchor the genre classification to several internal properties of the product (e.g., content, discourse structure, expression qualities) and their relationships;
- to reconstruct the designer's intentions inscribed within the multimedia product (this is the well-known design stance by Dennet [14]). This is helpful in order to understand a product's *technological mediation*, i.e., the way the product may affect the experience and the actions of the users [15]. This calls for a more responsible ethical attitude by the side of the designers and for a better awareness of the persuasive role of technologies by the side of users;
- to evaluate the authenticity of a product's brand by comparing the brand identity (i.e., the constellation of meanings-values the brand says to adhere to) with the actual meanings embodied and communicated by its marketing portfolio (e.g., video commercial).

III. A SEMIOTIC APPROACH

We address annotation by drawing on results obtained within the fields of semiotics and narratology [16] [17]. As stated by Scolari [17] Semiotics studies objects (texts, discourses) to understand processes (sense production and interpretation). It focuses on the meanings *inscribed* within a product and the *potential experience* that these meanings may trigger or evoke in the final users. It is both empirical and critical. It is based on the analysis of concrete products from a phenomenological perspective and is aimed at re-constructing the experiential project - a reading proposal or contract - that has been implicitly inscribed into the product by the designer-author starting from the product expression (i.e., its sensorial qualities) and explaining how semiotic materials (i.e., written text, images, music) and their combination may support such a project. From Semiotics we borrow the methodology of interpretive multimodal text analysis. Among the various semiotic research traditions that succeeded and stratified in time we are interested in those approaches that consider the meaning as the result of an interpretive process that can be articulated on different conceptual planes or layers. This is because we need a set of conceptualizations that could be used to build the means/ends ladder that we are looking for. Therefore we have taken as a reference the Generative Semiotic of Text by Greimas [18] [19] which we have integrated with some contributions coming from Socio Semiotics [20] and Enunciation Theory [18]. We propose to use the term "*Semiotic Annotation*" instead of the more commonplace term "*Semantic Annotation*" to emphasize this kind of approach. Looking at a video - and more generally at a multimedia product - from a semiotic point of view requires a new perspective on annotation. We consider the video presentation - i.e., the real time succession of multimodal events occurring during the interpretation-execution of digital data and instruction by a HW-SW platform - as a structured whole of *signs* (or semiotic resources) belonging to several *representational modalities* (e.g., written and spoken language, image, music, sound, audiovisual). These signs play the role of annotated data and the meanings referring to configuration of sensorial qualities of signs (expression), and arrangement of semantic entities (narrative content) as annotating data. In other words we annotate the flow of events as occurring during the execution of the presentation with the experiential (e.g., sensorial, narrative and relational-emotional) project envisaged by the designer and inscribed by her into the product [6]. We stress the fact that these meanings are always context sensitive and depend on the socio-cultural environment of the interpreter. Moreover, the intended meanings could be different from those attributed by the actual user if she does not correspond to the implied user (called the addressee). Only when the actual user projects herself into the implied one (i.e., there is a cooperation between sender and receiver) it can be said that the communication is truly effective.

IV. REQUIREMENTS FOR SEMIOTIC ANNOTATION

In this section, we present a list of requirements for the design of a semiotic compliant narrative video annotation. We have aggregated the requirements into three main classes namely: syntactic, semantic and pragmatic requirements. At the *syntactic level*, the conceptualization should enable the annotator:

- to structurally decompose the video presentation using different spatio-temporal *aggregation levels* and *conceptual abstractions*. As an instance, it should be possible to look at the video as a spatial configuration of regions within single key frames, or as a temporal sequence of individual shots, scenes, sequences, episodes, etc. Moreover, it should be possible to look at the video in terms of low level features; patterns of features (e.g., visual figures) that support a semantic construct such as an object, event or symbolic association; configurations of objects, subjects and events representing more abstract constructs such as situations, entire discourses and stories;
- to relate together the annotations pertaining to the *same/different* aggregation levels or conceptual abstractions by several types of relationships (e.g., spatial, temporal, logical, rhetorical, typological, mereological, causal/teleological relationships);
- to have multiple alternative annotations describing the presentation from different points of view (e.g., multiple coexisting alternative discourses/stories).

At the *semantic level*, the conceptualization should enable the annotator:

- to describe basic kinetic and plastic features of visual segments (e.g., shapes, colours, positions, textures, sizes, cinematic movements, visual contrasts, rhythms, etc.) as well as spectro-morphological features of audio segments (e.g., time features such as amplitude, envelope, etc. and spectral ones such as pitch, timbre, harmonicity);
- to represent meta-attributes such as for example aesthetic impressions (e.g., visual balance, order, symmetry) and product character [21];
- to describe representational meanings such as figurative formants in conceptual and narrative images [20]. More specifically to describe narrative structures by specifying all fundamental entities constituting a storyworld such as participants, actions, goals, settings [22]. To represent stories at different abstraction levels and using different dramaturgical schemas (e.g., the canonical scheme of Greimas [18], or the Hero's Journey by Campbell [23])

At the *pragmatic level*, the conceptualization should enable the annotator:

- to describe the interpersonal meaning associated to the presentation. As an instance, it should be possible to annotate the presentation with data regarding the inscribed addresser and addressee (i.e., the simulacra of the empirical sender/ receiver); their relationship, their attitude with reference to the content of the presentation, the intended effect the author wants to evoke in the actual receiver such as affective responses (emotions, mood, feelings);
- to describe the subjects of discourse (i.e., the subjects that are responsible for *how* a story is narrated and expressed by a text) and their relationships both with the characters of the story and the simulacra of the sender/receiver;
- to represent the deep values intended by the author (e.g., brand values) and the way they are inscribed within the video product.

Finally, the conceptualization should provide the annotator with a set of relationships that can be used to link all the above aspects together in order to build the desired means/ends ladder: deep values with storyline, the elements of the story with discourse segments and expressive qualities; expressive qualities with impressions and interpersonal meanings and so forth. We have recently proposed an informal conceptualization - not yet an ontology - that provides a core set of basic descriptors that can be used to perform a semiotic annotation according to the above requirements [24].

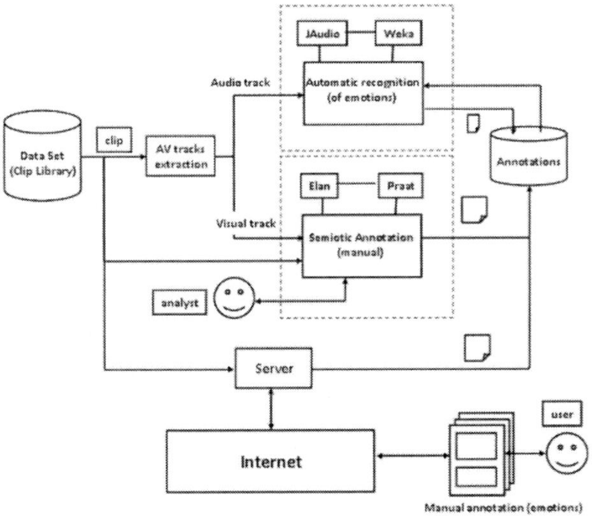

Figure 1. A schematic view of the infrastructure developed for video annotation

Figure 1 shows a conceptual model of an infrastructure we are developing to provide various kinds of automatic and manual annotation services. Currently, semiotic annotation is performed manually by expert annotators using the EUDICO Linguistic Annotator (*ELAN*) environment [25].

We are using this tool to make a series of annotation experiments whose aim is to assess the effectiveness of the conceptualization proposed in [24] and to create a preliminary data base of annotated resources that could be used in the future as a *ground truth* for automatic annotation algorithms. Automatic annotation is currently limited to the emotions expressed by audio tracks. It is performed by using jAudio and specific supervised learning techniques provided by Weka. Non-expert annotation of emotions in videos can be performed manually by users using mobile devices. Users' annotations provide data for the learning stage of the automatic annotation subsystem. In the next section we will illustrate in detail an example of expert annotation using *ELAN*.

V. A CASE STUDY

ELAN is a multimodal annotation tool that is widely used within the domain of Multimodal Discourse Analysis [26]. It enables the annotator to define a reference vocabulary and use it to describe an audiovisual product at different aggregation and abstraction levels (called annotation tiers). An annotation tier can be either alignable or referring. *Alignable tiers* are directly linked to the time axis of an audiovisual clip and can be divided into segments; *referring tiers* contain annotations that are linked to annotations on another tier which is called a parent tier and can be alignable or referring. Thus, tiers form a hierarchy where the root must be an alignable tier. The tool saves annotations in the XML format based on *ELAN* XML Schema. For the analysis of the audio component in the temporal and spectral domains the *Praat* software has been used [27]. *Pratt* results can be imported within *ELAN* and easily integrated with visual annotations.

In order to provide an example of semiotic annotation we will focus here on an advertisement clip by Pepsi-Cola [28]. The clip produced in the late 1980's is based on the bodycopy "Pepsi Cola. The choice of a new generation". A delivery van of Pepsi Cola reaches a crowded beach. The young driver gets out, opens the side door and switches an amplifier on; two loudspeakers emerge from the roof of the van. The boy brings a bottle of Pepsi near the microphone, uncaps it, pours liquid into a glass and drinks emitting an "Ahhhh" of pleasure. People attracted by puffing of gas and the boy's expression rush to the van to quench their thirst.

A systematic procedure has been envisaged for the analysis and annotation of video commercials (and more generally of audiovisual products). The procedure consists of the following basic stages:

- Stage-0 (*Whole clip annotation*). The whole clip is represented by an alignable annotation tier linked to a single segment (ClipSegment). This tier represents the root of the hierarchical multi-tiers annotation. In the case of the Pepsi Cola clip the ClipSegment last 29.5s at the frame rate of 30fps. The tier is annotated with the multimedia genre and the intention/goal of the product. In this way the genre and goal are directly linked with other annotations.
- Stage-1 (*Textual decomposition*). The root segment (ClipSegment) is represented by several textual structures (T-Structure). Some structures are associated to the visual representation modality, others to the aural modality. In the considered example, a structure (T-Structure1) is used to decompose ClipSegment into a sequence of T-Segments representing individual shots. By the term shot we intend a series of visual frames produced by the camera in an uninterrupted recording operation. A further textual structure (T-Structure2) is used to annotate special transition edits and effects like fades, dissolves, overlayed text, etc. Finally, another structure (T-Structure3) is used to decompose the ClipSegment on the base of continuous sequences (T-Segments) of homogeneous sound objects. In the Pepsi example these sequences include silence, speech, environmental sound and effects. In more complex examples it could be necessary to devote a separate textual structure to each constituent of a complex audio sandwich e.g., music, effects, speeches, environmental sounds as well as to sound transitions. It should be stressed that visual and aural structures are not necessarily aligned in time. Speech and music for example can continue while the camera switches from one shot to the next one.
- Stage-2 (*Textual annotation*). In this stage a set of referring annotation tiers are introduced and associated to previous visual and aural structures to annotate single shots, transitions and sound objects with tonal and rhythmic sensorial qualities such as colour, shape, texture, timbre, pitch, movement, tempo, etc. Further tiers can be used to annotate intended hedonic impressions (e.g., emotions, mood), and meta-attributes (e.g., product character).
- Stage-3 (*Discourse decomposition*). The root ClipSegment is represented by one or more discourse structures (D-Structure). The decomposition is based on *scene* analysis. A scene (D-Segment) is defined as a - not necessarily continuous - sequence of frames representing a narrative situation characterized by a stable setting (i.e., place, time and mise-en-scene). In the case under consideration, we use a single discourse structure (D-Structure1) which is decomposed into 17 D-Segments. Scene boundaries corresponds to changes in settings from outside to inside the Pepsi Cola van and vice-versa.
- Stage-4 (*Narrative structure decomposition*). Each scene (D-Segment) is annotated by a narrative structure composed by narrative programs [18] [19] and their logical and temporal relationships.
- Stage-5 (*Narrative program annotation*). A set of referring annotation tiers are introduced and associated to previous narrative structures to annotate single narrative programs. For each narrative program a set of tiers is used to separately

describe the main components of the program namely the actor (subject of doing), the action, the effect (subject of state, transition) and the object of value. In the example under consideration, D-Segment7 and D-Segment9 (a scene inside van) is annotated by a narrative structure composed by the temporal sequence of two narrative programs. The first program (D-NP4) refers to the boy (D-Agent) grasping the bottle of Pepsi (D-Action) thus making user aware of brand (D-effect). The second narrative program (D-NP5) refers again to the boy (D-Agent) who uncaps the bottle and pours drinks content (D-Action) thus getting object of value, i.e., the product/brand (D-Effect).

- Stage-6 (*Relational analysis and annotation*). The root segment (ClipSegment) is analyzed in order to identify the markers of addresser and addressee. As an example, in the Pepsi Cola clip, the bottle of Pepsi including the logo and trademark represents the addresser (i.e., the brand Pepsi). The people approaching the van to buy the product is a representation (a surrogate) of the addressee. A set of further tiers have been introduced and linked to the ClipSegment to represent interpersonal metafunctions [20] expressed by visual and aural features. According to social semiotics, a character's gaze, size of shot, vertical and horizontal camera angle, are related to engagement, social distance, power and involvement relationships respectively. In the same way, tone of voice in speech, sound perspective, volume, can be used to evoke various degrees of intimacy or distance between the characters of the story (and indirectly the brand) and the user. The clip aims at establishing both empathy and trust between users/consumers and actors. Empathy can occur between the boy and the user, which is urged to share with crowds the sensation of freshness. The user is also invited to trust that the experience ensured by brand Pepsi – the addresser – is authentic; that drink (and indirectly the brand) is indeed an object of value in that context, so worthwhile purchasing.

Several temporal relationships among annotations belonging to different tiers are implicitly described through the relations existing between their corresponding tiers. For example, all referring tiers associated to the same alignable tier inherit its time decomposition. As a consequence their annotations are automatically time aligned. Figure 2 shows a screen shot of ELAN illustrating a subset of the tiers used to annotate the Pepsi Cola clip.

VI. DISCUSSION

It is important to recognize that semiotic annotation is model based: it exploits a meta-model (i.e., an informal ontology) of the narrative video genre. The meta-model [24] makes explicit different assumptions, conceptualizations and theories shared within the semiotic field. One assumption is that the realization of a commercial video amounts to the construction of meaning and that the meaning rests on the relationships existing between the text, discourse and story layers rather than on the single elements of the video.

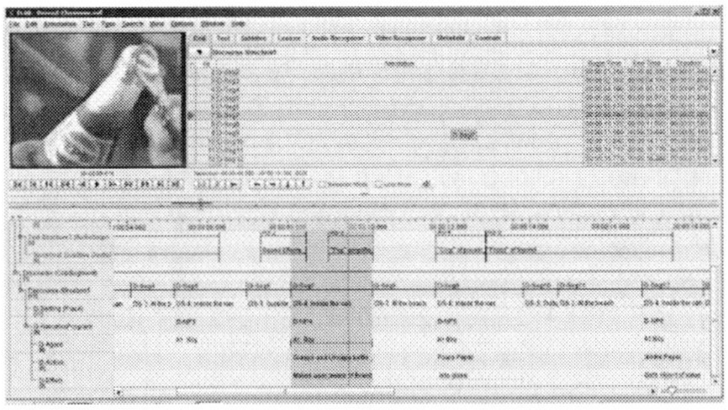

Figure 2. A screenshot of *ELAN* representing a subset of annotation tiers associated to the Pepsi Cola clip.

These relationships provide the video with the kind of unity, internal coherence and sense it shows. As a consequence, as discussed in the Section IV, the meta-model is multi-layered and relational. In this context, the annotation represents a kind of *intermediate level knowledge* [29], connecting the abstract concepts of the ontology, that are used, as descriptors, in the annotation, to the specific values these concepts take in the concrete video under consideration. Under this perspective, the annotation unfolds the design knowledge that is embodied in the artifact. It shows how the meta-model has been instantiated by the author of the video in the concrete artifact.

The availability of design knowledge provides several benefits for the designers and the users as well. It allows to answer several questions about the product. These questions - that are the *competence questions* associated to the ontology - refer, for example, to the way a narrative is decomposed into narrative programs; how a specific narrative program has been translated at the textual level (in terms of visual and auditory qualities); who is involved in the story (as well as in discourse) and which functional role he/she is playing (e.g., subject of action, subject of value, simulacrum of the sender/receiver, narrator, and so forth); how social distance and involvement are evoked through the visual and the auditory features (e.g., by selection of shot size, direction of the eye gaze, horizontal and vertical position of video camera; or by selection of sonic perspective, panorama, pitch distribution, etc.). The annotation can be used for search and retrieval (e.g., search all videos or parts of videos where a specific narrative program is represented or where a specific social distance is employed) but we think that design knowledge inscribed within the annotation is fundamentally useful for explaining the way a specific video functions from a communicative point of view: how meaning is constructed - in *that* video - by the interplay of several elements located at different levels of the means-end semiotic ladder. For designers, in particular, the annotation affords extraction of the design knowledge embodied within the video in order to reuse it, evaluate its internal coherence or take inspiration from it in developing new products. They can exploit the annotation to compare two or more video of the same author or brand in order to search for redundancies and variations. They can aggregate videos on the base of similarities in the way they function (i.e., how they instantiate the meta-model) with the goal of constructing portfolios or exhibitions. This may benefit several target users such as, for example, artists, architects, industrial designers. For generic users, the annotation presents a more fundamental benefit. It is known that every artifact - and technology, in general - plays a *mediation* role: it changes the way users perceive and experience the world as well as the way they act in the world [30]. The mediation effect is usually made transparent, in the sense that is not visible. However, recent studies in the field of Philosophy of Technology claim that such an effect should be made opaque and comprehensible to users [31]. In the case of advertisement products - such as the video commercials - this means to make explicit the rhetorical mechanisms that are at the base of their persuasive and informative functioning. This is useful for the user in order to better understand how the video has been designed to satisfy the author's intended goals, why it functions as it does, what sort of culture it will encourage or resist. Moreover, the disclosure of motivations, methods, and intended outcomes is one of the ethical principles in persuasive design as discussed in [32]. Semiotic annotation may support this principle and contribute to the diffusion of a critical attitude toward multimedia and a greater awareness of the social effects this kind of products may produce.

In the specific case study under consideration, semiotic annotation is useful to explain how the Pepsi Cola video functions. The video tries to persuade to consume the Pepsi Cola by means of a narrative telling us "the process of persuasion of buying/consuming a Pepsi Cola". This process includes the following steps: 1) insert yourself in a familiar situation (the delivery van of the Pepsi Cola reaches the crowded beach); 2) draw attention and represent a positive and euphoric experience of consumption (loudspeakers attract people; the experience of the boy drinking the Pepsi is communicated both visually and auditory); 3) activate in the consumer a desire to have a similar experience through the planning and realization of a purchase behavior (people rush to the van to buy the Pepsi). The persuasive goal is realized through three types of relationships: between the user and the product; between the user and the subject using the product, and, finally, between the user and the people-crowd on the beach that desire the product and activate themself to buy it. It is sufficient to view and hear the protagonist (the boy) uncapping the bottle, drinking the liquid and emitting the "Ahhhh" of pleasure to activate, in the user and in the crowd, a similar experience on the base of a common competence of what does it means to drink a cold beverage. Semiotic annotation allows the annotator to associate the shots of the video to the various phases of the persuasive process; to describe each shots by representing its associated narrative programs and visual and auditory qualities; to describe the technical and discursive mechanisms that are used to address the user and to engage him/her; to evaluate the degree of verisimilitude associated to the video by analyzing the kinds of sound objects that are used and the use of subjective or objective shots; etc.

Semiotic annotation is different from pure keyword or concept annotation. The task is not simply to attach subjective comments, notes, interpretations or remarks to audiovisual segments but to unfold the generative process of sense making inscribed within the product. As a consequence the annotation should be performed by the video author since he/she is in a privileged position to provide valuable knowledge about design decisions. Alternatively, it could be made by other subjects such as critics or commentators, preferably with the help of the author. Anyway, the annotation should be considered as a constitutive part of the video. Through its indexical nature it points to features of the video and connects them to general concepts and issues making them topical for further discussion. It adds value to the product since it supports interpretation, clarification and comprehension.

One critical question regards the complexity of the task. Semiotic annotation requires deep knowledge about semiotic theories and well developed analytical skills. Part of this expert knowledge is embodied in the meta-model [24] that provides the relevant conceptualizations and vocabularies for the description. This is a benefit with respect to more general (i.e., not model-based) approaches. Automatic tools can be used to support low level analysis of expressive qualities such as shot detection, dominant colour identification, spectro-morphological analysis of sound objects, basic video statistics, etc. However, for the more abstract levels, the human intervention is still needed.

Manual annotation is time-consuming but our experience showed that, for video commercials, it is a feasible approach due to the limited time extension of these kinds of texts. The effort, in this case, is largely rewarded by the benefits connected with the unfolding of new design knowledge as discussed beforehand. For longer texts such as films and documentaries the manual approach is surely unfeasible without appropriate supporting tools. This is a direction of possible future research work. A final remark regards the scope of applicability of semiotic annotation. Although semiotic theories can be fruitfully applied for the analysis of a wide range of genres of texts (and recently to physical artifacts as well) we consider persuasive discourses (such as video commercials, advertising images, learning objects and advergames) the most interesting fields of application. The rationale is that these kinds of texts are *intentionally* developed to affect the experience and behavior of the intended users so they are usually carefully designed to achieve these persuasive goals. Therefore, it is particularly interesting to unfold the design thinking embodied in such types of products.

VII. Conclusions

This paper focuses on annotation of video commercials viewed as mediators between the intention of the designer/author and the interpretation of the user.

The main contributions can be summarized as follows:

- a new concept of annotation called semiotic annotation has been proposed to support means/ends description of video texts. The concept emphasizes the multilayered and interrelated nature of meanings embedded within the product. More specifically, a (narrative) video is conceived of as a structured system composed by three interrelated layers: story (*what* is depicted in the product), discourse (*how* it is told) and text (how the discourse is manifested through multimodal resources) [33];
- a systematic method has been outlined that can be used to manually annotate commercial video using *ELAN* as the annotation tool and the informal ontology proposed in [24] as the source of descriptors. The empirical annotation work done with the *ELAN* tool has showed the effectiveness of the proposed conceptual framework. A formalization of the conceptualization using *Protégé* is under development. The aim is to build an OWL-2 ontology that can be linked to DOLCE and could support a rich set of competency questions not currently supported by the simple query engine by *ELAN*.

Semiotic methods of analysis and descriptions are currently under utilized in the field of multimedia semantic annotation [10]. This paper strives for being a preliminary step toward a more "semiotic aware" attitude in this field.

REFERENCES

[1] CISCO, "Cisco Visual Networking Index: Forecast and Methodology, 2015-2020," White Paper, Cisco, 2016.

[2] IAB, "Digital Video In-Stream Ad Format Guidelines," Interactive Advertising Bureau, 2016.

[3] C. G. M. Snoek, and M. Worring, "Multimodal video indexing: a review of the state-of-the-art," Multimedia Tools and Applications, Vol. 25, pp. 5-35, 2005.

[4] N. Crilly, A. Maier, and P. J. Clarkson, "Representing artifacts as media: modelling the relationship between designer intent and consumer experience," Journal of Design, Vol. 2, No.3, pp.15–27, 2008.

[5] T. M. Karjalainen, "It looks like a Toyota: Educational approaches to Designing for visual brand recognition," International Journal of Design, Vol.1, No.1, pp. 67-81, 2007.

[6] R. Eugeni, "Media Experiences and practices of analysis. For a critical pragmatics of media," International Workshop "Practicing Theory", University of Amsterdam, March 2-4, 2011.

[7] E. Oren, K. H. Moller, S. Scerri, S. Handschuh, and M. Sintek, "What are Semantic Annotations," Technical Report, DERI, Galway, 2006.

[8] J. M. Martinez, "MPEG-7 Overview," ISO/IEC JTC1/SC29/WG11 N6828, Palma de Mallorca, Spain, 2004.

[9] A. B. Benitez, J. M. Martinez, H. Rising, and P. Salembier, "Description of a single multimedia document," in Introduction to MPEG 7: Multimedia Content Description Language," B.S.Manjunath, P.Salembier, T.Sikora (Eds.), Wiley, pp.111-138, 2002.

[10] R. Troncy, B. Huet, and S. Schenk, Multimedia Semantics, Metadata, Analysis and Interaction, Wiley, 2011.

[11] J. Bardzell, and S. Bardzell, "Interaction criticism: a proposal and framework for a new discipline of HCI," Proc. CHI2008, ACM, New York, USA, pp. 2463-2472, 2008.

[12] P. Wright, J. Wallace, and J. McCarthy, "Aesthetic and experience-centered design," ACM Transactions on Computer-Human Interaction, Vol.15, No.4, Article 18, 2008.

[13] G. Cockton, "When and Why feelings and impressions matter in Interaction Design," Invited keynote address, Proc. Kansei 2009, Warsawa, Poland, 2009.

[14] N. Crilly, "The design stance in user-system interaction," Design Issues, Vol. 27, No. 4, pp. 16-29, 2011.

[15] L. Anticoli, and E. Toppano, "Technological mediation of ontologies: the need for tools to help designers in materializing ethics," International Journal of Philosophy Study, Vol.1, Issue 3, pp. 23-31, 2013.

[16] C. Bianchi, "Semiotic approaches to advertising texts and strategies: narrative, passion, marketing," Semiotica 183, 1/4, pp. 243-271, 2011.

[17] C. Scolari, "Transmedia storytelling: Implicit consumers, narrative worlds, and branding in contemporary media production," International Journal of Communication, Vol.3. pp. 586–606, 2009.

[18] A. J. Greimas, and P. Courtès, Semiotics and language. An analytical dictionary, Indiana University Press, Bloomington, IN, 1982.

[19] E. Toppano, and V. Roberto, "Semiotic Design and Analysis of Hypermedia," in Proc. 20th ACM Conference on Hypertext and Hypermedia, HT2009, Turin, Italy, 367-368, 2009.

[20] G. Kress, and T. van Leeuwen, Reading images. The grammar of visual design. Routledge, New York, 2003.

[21] L. Janlert, and E. Stolterman, "The character of things," Design Studies, Vol. 18, No. 3, pp. 297-314, 1997.

[22] M. L. Ryan, "Narrativity and its modes as culture-trascending analytical categories," Japan Forum, 21(3), BAJS, pp. 307–323, 2009.

[23] J. Campbell, The hero with a thousand faces. New World Library, 2008.

[24] E. Toppano, and V. Roberto, "Semiotic-based conceptual modelling of Hypermedia," Proc. Image Analysis and Processing, ICIAP2013, Napoli, Italy, Lecture Notes in Computer Science, Vol. 8157, pp. 663-672, 2013.

[25] B. Hellwing, and D. Uytvanck, "EUDICO Linguistic Annotator (ELAN)," Version 2.0.2, software manual, 2004.

[26] K. L. O'Halloran, Multimodal discourse analysis. In K. Hyland and B. Paltridge (eds.) Companion to Discourse, London and New York: Continuum, 2011.

[27] P. Boersmimedia a, and D. Weenink, "Praat: doing phonetics by computer," available from: http://www.fon.hum.uva.nl/

[28] Pepsi Cola clip [online]. Available from: http://www.youtube.com/watch?v=edfRG9lREHc Accessed: 2 february 2017.

[29] J. Lowgren, "Annotated Portfolios and other form of Intermediate-Level Knowledge," Interactions, pp. 30-34, 2013.

[30] P. P. Verbeek, "Materializing Morality: Design Ethics and Technological Mediation," Science, Technology & Human Values, Vol. 31, No. 3, pp. 361- 380, 2006.

[31] Y. Van Den Eede, "In between us: on the transparency and opacity of Technological Mediation," Found. Sci. 16, pp.139-159, 2011.

[32] D. Berdichevski, and E. Neuenschwander, "Toward an Ethics of Persuasive Technology," Communication of the ACM, Vol. 45, No. 5, pp. 51-58, 1999.

[33] N. J. Lowe, "A cognitive model," in Bernstein, M., and Gerco D. (Eds.) Reading Hypertext, Eastgate Systems, 2009.

ModRef Project: from Creation to Exploitation of CIDOC-CRM Triplestores

Pascaline Tchienehom

Université de Paris 10 - Labex "Les passés dans le présent"
Nanterre, France
Email: pkenfack@u-paris10.fr

***Abstract*—ModRef is a project from the laboratory Labex "Les passés dans le présent", which coordinates various projects on digital humanities. ModRef focuses more precisely on the semantic web and linked open data. The goal is to move heterogeneous data into triplestores also called data warehouses or collections of RDF files in order to improve the sharing, exchange and discovery of new knowledge. For this purpose, the CIDOC-CRM norm has been chosen since it is, at present, the reference for the semantic description of museographic data or cultural heritage data. In order to realise the proof of concept of ModRef, a general architecture has been defined, a semantic modelling and data mapping of selected sub-projects of ModRef have been proposed, triplestores have also been created. A web application has been implemented and deployed. This web application describes the ModRef project, as well as it enables visualising, querying and exploring created triplestores.**

Keywords–Digital Humanities; Semantic Web; Linked Open Data; Triplestores; CIDOC-CRM.

I. Introduction

The laboratory Labex "Les passés dans le présent" accompanies several projects in Social and Human Sciences (SHS) on issues related to digital humanities [1]: from dematerialisation of data to their structural description and even to their semantic description as well. ModRef (Modelling, References and Digital Culture) is a project from Labex that gather together a set of sub-projects with the goal of migrating their data into triplestores or data warehouses or collections of RDF (Resource Description Framework) files in order to improve the sharing, exchange and discovery of new knowledge. For this purpose, the CIDOC-CRM (International Committee for DOCumentation-Conceptual Reference Model) norm [2] has been chosen because it is currently the reference for the semantic description of museographic data or cultural heritage data [3]. The aim is globally to move from non-structured or semi-structured data to structured data and afterwards from structured data to semantic data. The semantic web then provides a solution to perform these data migrations.

The semantic web [4][5] is not only a concept but also an architecture [6], which is increasingly used in several applications. The semantic web architecture is a set of independant layers that collaborate to perform various tasks. This architecture describes data from their representation to their exploitation by applications or semantic web agents. Hence, various norms of data representation exist. The CIDOC-CRM is an example of semantic norm and more precisely a conceptual reference model. The aim of semantics and also the aim of the various metadata languages or semantic norms that define semantics is to provide an homogenous framework for representing and querying heterogenous data in order to reduce information silence and therefore improve the discovery of knowledge. Hence, ModRef project aims at realising a migration of data towards CIDOC-CRM triplestores using core data originally from heterogenous data sources where heterogeneity is based on contents and initial logical structure (spreadsheets, relational databases, XML files) as well.

In this paper, we present the ModRef project through: a general description of the CIDOC-CRM norm, in section 2; the general architecture of the ModRef project, in section 3; a CIDOC-CRM semantic modelling and data mapping of the three pilot sub-projects of ModRef with the CIDOC-CRM graph, in section 4; a migration of data into CIDOC-CRM triplestores, in section 5; a visualisation and exploitation of triplestores through the web application [7] that has been developped and deployed, in section 6; the evaluation procedure and results, in section 7.

II. CIDOC-CRM General Presentation

There are various data representation models based on semantics [8][9] that use metadata languages to describe concepts and/or links (properties or predicates) between concepts or instances of concepts (Dublin Core, RDF, RDFS, OWL, FOAF, Wordnet, CIDOC-CRM). The *CIDOC-CRM* [2] is a conceptual reference model for describing museographic data or cultural heritage data. The version of the CIDOC-CRM norm that we have worked with is the version 6.2 of may 2015. It describes 94 classes and 168 properties. In 2006, the CIDOC-CRM has become a norm ISO 21127:2006 but work on that norm has started since 1996. This norm describes general characteristics of objects (identifier, type, title, material, dimension, note) but also history of objects through events or activities (transfer of custody -former localisations, current localisation-, origin, discovery, curation, attribute assignement, measurement), as well as relations between objects or parts of objects (bibliography, composition, similarity, other representation -photo, drawing, painting-, inscription). An OWL implementation of the CIDOC-CRM by the University of Erlangen-Nuremberg is available [10] and the namespace of that implementation of CIDOC-CRM is usually prefixed by "*ecrm*".

The general structure of the CIDOC-CRM is described in Figure 1. The root class of all CIDOC-CRM entities is the class *E1 CRM Entity* and it is subdivided in direct sub-classes, among which the two main classes are:

1) *E77 Persistent Item*, which is the generic class of persistent entities. A persistent entity is an entity that can survive over an indeterminate time, such as:

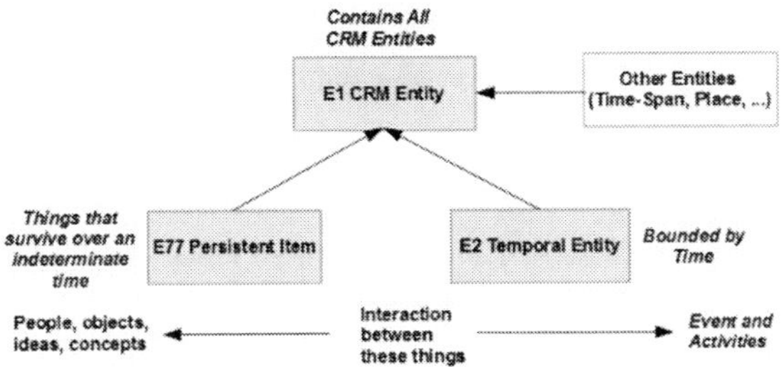

Figure 1. General Structure of CIDOC-CRM Entities.

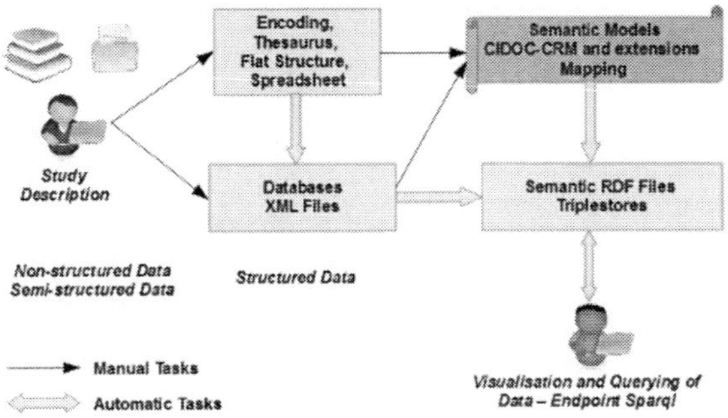

Figure 2. Architecture of ModRef project.

persons, objects, ideas, concepts. Those entities can have a beginning or an end of existence;

2) *E2 Temporal Entity*, which is the generic class of temporal entities. A temporal entity is an entity bounded by time (with a beginning and an end time), such as: event, beginning of existence, end of existence, activity, creation, production, modification, transfer of custody, curation, attribute assignement, measurement.

The other direct sub-classes of the root class *E1 CRM Entity* are the classes *E52 Time-Span, E53 Place, E54 Dimension, E92 Spacetime Volume*. In general, the CIDOC-CRM describes entities but also interactions that can exist between entities: interactions between persistent entities; interactions between temporal entities; interactions between persistent and temporal entities; general interactions between entities (for instance, interactions that exist between persistent or temporal entities and other general entities describing time-span, place, dimension). There also exists interactions between entities and primitive values (string, number, date time).

Besides, various projects around the world work on the migration of data into triplestores (CIDOC-CRM or not):

1) The *British Museum* [11], which is a museum on history and culture and that uses the CIDOC-CRM;
2) *Arches* [12], which is a collaboration between the Getty Conservation Institute (GCI) and the World Monuments Fund (WMF) on immovable cultural heritage (monuments, bridges) and that uses the CIDOC-CRM;
3) *DBPedia* [13], which is an online encyclopedia widely used [14] and that does not use the CIDOC-CRM norm but various metadata languages, such as: *dbpedia, foaf, umbel, schema.org, dublin core, geo*;
4) *Nakala* [15], which is an online service to upload, document and exhibit (museographic) data and that does not use the CIDOC-CRM norm but various metadata languages, such as: *foaf, skos, dublin core, vcard.*

The specificity of our web application is that it deals with heterogeneous data sources according to the contents and the logical structures (spreadsheets, relational databases, XML files) of data. Data migrated into triplestores are opened through our web application. This application provides a visualisation service of triplestores under three differents formats: *rdf, triples, attribute-value summary*. The web application also allows querying triplestores seperately or together by using *"Endpoint Sparql"* (interface for typing and executing Sparql query, where Sparql is a querying language for RDF files) and *general query forms* that are useful for those who do not know the Sparql query language [16] and the CIDOC-CRM language.

III. ARCHITECTURE OF THE MODREF PROJECT

The architecture of the ModRef project, illustrated in Figure 2, describes the various processes of data digitisation from the creation of digital data based on an expert knowledge for instance to the visualisation and querying of data by a user. Data can go through several transformations before being available in triplestores. Hence, we can move from non-structured or semi-structured data (notes, reports, books, web sites) to structured data described by logical structure. This logical structure can be a flat structure of the form *attribute-value* or *spreadsheet*, but it can also be more structured using *relational databases* or *XML files* that are, in our context, XML-EAD (Encoded Archival Description) files [17]. These various descriptions usually make use of thesaurus (controlled vocabulary of descriptive terms or not). From those structural descriptions, we can build a semantic description of data with a semantic RDF graph which relies on standards or norms. In our context, we have used the CIDOC-CRM norm to generate triplestores through a mapping between data and the CIDOC-CRM graph. These triplestores can then be used by semantic web applications or "Endpoint Sparql". The first stage of data transformation (from non-structured or semi-structured data towards structured data) is performed within each sub-project of ModRef whereas ModRef project itself focuses more on the second stage of data transformation (from structured data to semantic data).

Therefore, to realise the proof of concept (POC) of ModRef, three pilot projects have been selected:

1) *CDLI (Cuneiform Digital Library Initiative)*: Digital museum on antique documents in cuneiform writing [18];
2) *ObjMythArcheo*: corpus of antique archaeological objects with mythological iconography [19];
3) *BiblioNum*: Digital library on history of France during the 20th century [20].

Table I compares data of the three pilot projects of ModRef based on 5 criteria: descriptive texts size, number of objects, logical structure type, number of elements of the logical structure and data description language.

TABLE I. DATA COMPARISON.

	CDLI	ObjMythArcheo	BiblioNum
Texts size	300 Mo	100 Mo	100 Mo
Number of objects	313 332 objects	17 424 objects	77 collections - 62 392 files
Logical Structure	Database of type Spreadsheet	Relational Database	XML-EAD
Number of elements of the structure	1 table with 61 attributes	59 tables	146 XML-EAD elements
Language	English	French-English	French

IV. MODREF CIDOC-CRM MODELLING AND DATA MAPPING

We have identified the useful CIDOC-CRM classes, for which at least one path leads to a non-null value, for the data modelling of our three pilot projects. This modelling represents extracts related to the four following themes or subjects:

1) general characteristics of objects (identifier, type, title, material, dimension, note or description), bibliography, composition and similarity of objects;
2) events of beginning of existence (origin) and end of existence;
3) miscellaneous activities (transfer of custody, attribute assignement, measurement);
4) inscriptions and other representations (photo, drawing, painting).

In general, those extracts are constant because with the CIDOC-CRM, it is possible to identify all potential paths that lead to a given information. A semantic graph is thus a set of nodes and oriented arrows that fulfill some constraints and rules (shortcut, entailment, inverse). These constraints and rules define the consistency and validity of the model.

In the following sections, we will describe the four different themes (graph's extracts) for the CIDOC-CRM modelling of our pilot projects and also an instance of data mapping with the corresponding CIDOC-CRM semantic graph snippet. Note that the mapping or alignment principle is globally the same for all themes and for all pilot projects.

A. Modelling of general characteristics

General characteristics of an object is defined more often by interactions through short graph's paths. Those characteristics describe for an object various information, such as: identifier, type (categorisation), title, material, dimension, note or general description.

The modelling of the general characteristics of objects of the ModRef project is illustrated in Figure 3. In this figure, there are two different graph's paths for defining the dimension of an object:

1) a *short path* or *shortcut path* that links class *E70 Thing* to class *E54 Dimension* with the property *P43 has dimension* by the triple *[E70 Thing, P43 has dimension, E54 Dimension]*;
2) a *long path* with more nodes to fill. This path is described by the following triples: *[E1 CRM Entity, P39i was measured by, E16 Measurement], [E16 Measurement, P40 observed dimension, E54 Dimension]*. With this path, we can fill more information related to the activity of measurement *E16 Measurement*. Actually, the class *E16 Measurement* is a type of activity because classes *E13 Attribute Assignment*, *E7 Activity* and *E5 Event* belong to its hierarchy (see Figure 4).

Besides, it is authorised to fill various paths leading to the same information in a CIDOC-CRM graph. Therefore, we sometimes have to choose between the different possibilities when we do not have the necessary information to describe a given path. This is the case mostly when a temporal entity is used in the path.

On the other hand, Figure 3 also illustrates other interactions between persistent entities, such as: *P70i is documented in* for bibliographic references, *P46 is composed of* for objects composition, *P130 shows features of* for objects similarity, *P128 carries* for relation between an object and an entity carried by or engraved on the described object, such as an inscription for example.

B. Modelling of events of beginning and end of existence

An important activity on museographic data is the description of their origin (beginning of existence) in order to define their date of origin, their place of origin and eventually the participants to their origin or creation. The modelling of beginning and end of existence events of objects in the ModRef project is illustrated in Figure 4. The CIDOC-CRM allows to define for each event three main information: date or period, place and participants.

For the beginning of existence (origin), we use the event *E63 Beginning of Existence* and the following patterns of triples: *[E77 Persistent Item, P92i was brought into existence by, E63 Beginning of Existence], [E2 Temporal Entity, P4 has time-span, E52 Time-Span], [E52 Time-Span, P78 is identified by, E49 Time Appellation], [E4 Period, P7 took place at, E53 Place], [E53 Place, P87 is identified by, E44 Place Appellation], [E5 Event, P11 had participant, E39 Actor], [E63 Beginning of Existence, rdfs : subClassOf, E5 Event], [E5 Event, rdfs : subClassOf, E4 Period], [E4 Period, rdfs : subClassOf, E2 Temporal Entity]*. Besides, for the beginning of existence (origin) we may also start from activities *E65 Creation* or *E12 Production*, which have as super-classes the classes *E63 Beginning of Existence* and *E7 Activity* (see Figure 4).

For the end of existence, we use the class *E64 End of Existence* or any of its sub-classes and we will then be able to define the date, the place and the participants to the end of existence of an object.

C. Modelling of miscellaneous activities

Figure 5 illustrates an extract of our model for the description of activities in general, and for the description of the activity *transfer of custody* in particular. Hence, to link an object to an activity of transfer of custody, we use the property *P30 transferred custody of* (or its inverse *P30i custody transferred through*) between the target activity (*E10 Transfer of Custody*) and the physical object (*E18 Physical Thing*). Moreover, for a transfer of custody, we can describe the various protagonists of the transfer (*P29 custody received by, P28 custody surrendered by*) and also describe eventually a history of the different transfers of custody related to a specific object or document. Note that, there also exists a shortcut path that does not use the transfer of custody activity but that allows to define the current or former keepers or owners of an object

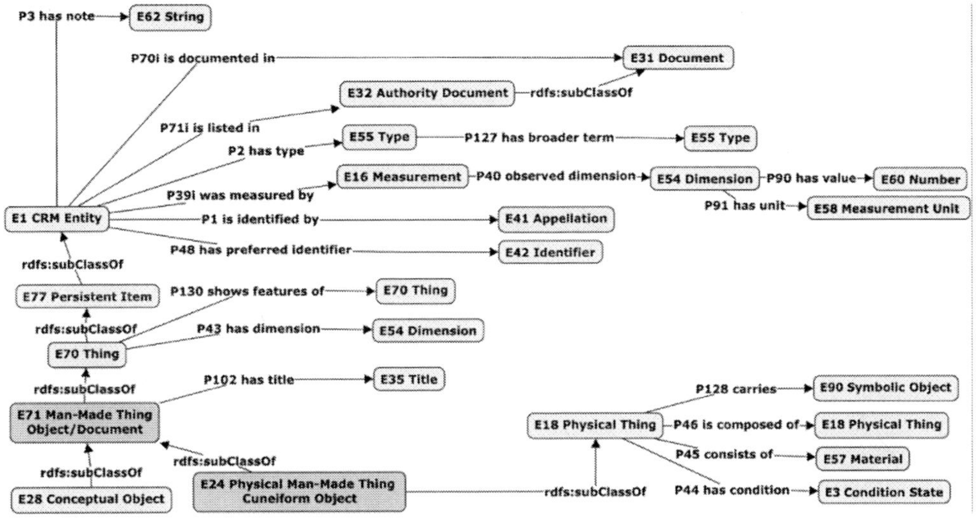

Figure 3. Modelling of general characteristics.

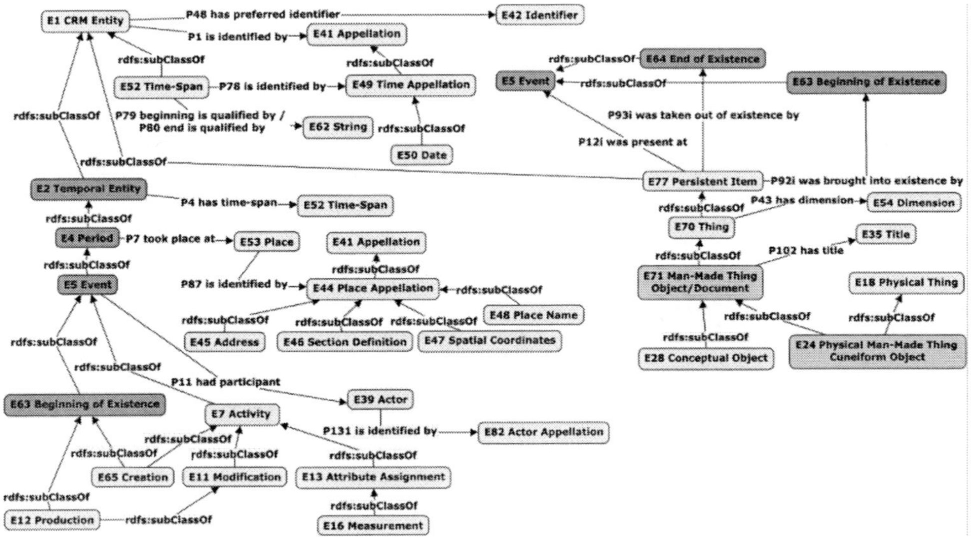

Figure 4. Modelling of events of beginning and end of existence.

(*P49 has former or current keeper, P50 has current keeper, P51 has former or current owner, P52 has current owner*).

Generally, for an event or an activity, we can describe the date (or period), the place and the participants (or actors) of the event or activity. Specifically, for an activity (transfer of custody, attribute assignement, measurement, curation), we will be able to define more information, such as: the procedure or technique used (*P33 used specific technique, P32 used general technique*), the various objects used (*P16 used specific object, P125 used object of type*), the purpose of the activity (*P20 had specific purpose, P21 had general purpose*).

D. Modelling of inscriptions and other representations

Figure 6 illustrates a snippet of the model for the description of inscriptions engraved on objects or the description of other representations (photo, drawing, painting) of these objects (physical or conceptual). Hence, to link an object to its inscription, we use the property *P128 carries* between a physical object (*E18 Physical Thing*) and a symbolic objet (*E90 Symbolic Object*) that is inscribed on the target described object. This will then help to find, for instance, all objects engraved with a given inscription (seal, signature).

Besides, to link a photo or drawing or painting to an object (physical or conceptual), we can use a set of properties:

1) *P62 depicts* for describing the link between the photo or drawing or painting (here, *E24 Physical Man-Made Thing*) and the target entity *E1 CRM Entity* (physical or conceptual object) represented by the photo, drawing or painting. This property does not describe inscriptions or other information engraved

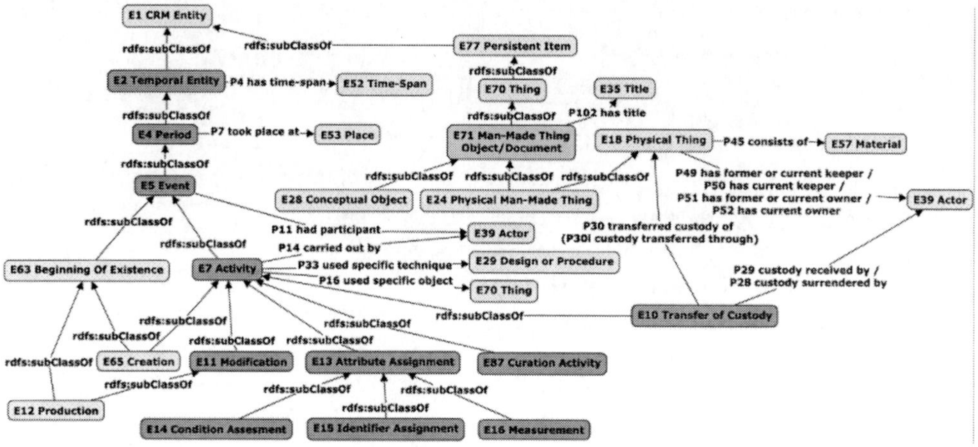

Figure 5. Modelling of miscellaneous activities.

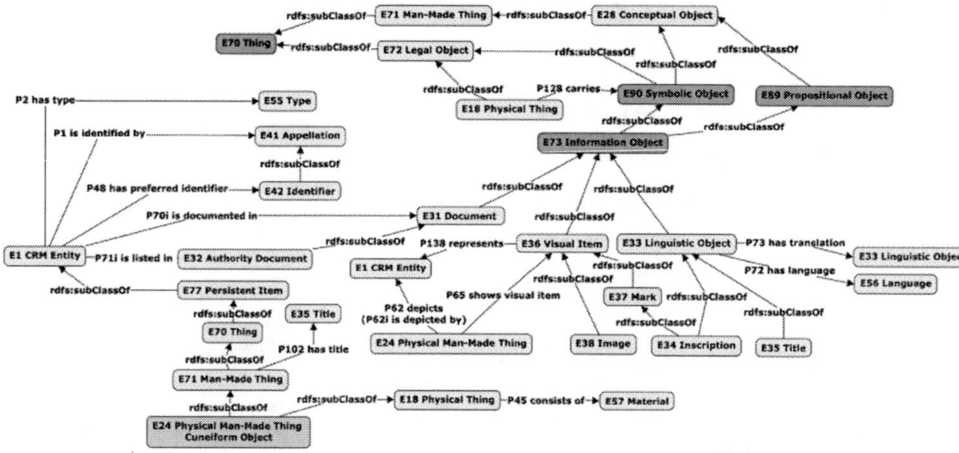

Figure 6. Modelling of inscriptions and other representations of an object.

directly on objects;

2) *P65 shows visual item* that links the photo or drawing or painting to a visual representation (*E36 Visual item*) of the described object represented by the photo or drawing or painting;
3) *P138 represents* that links a visual representation (*E36 Visual item*) of an object to the target described object (*E1 CRM Entity*).

Note that, the property *P62 depicts* is a shortcut of properties *P65 shows visual item* and *P138 represents*. The photo or drawing or painting is usually described with the class *E24 Physical Man-Made Thing*.

E. Data Mapping or Alignment

Data migration into triplestores requires an alignment stage of data with extracts of the CIDOC-CRM graph proposed. This mapping is essential due to the heterogeneity of initial data structured description and also due to the diversity of pilot projects. This matching is not properly a programmatic task but relies on logical structure details specific to the structural descriptive model chosen by each sub-project. It is a task halfway between modelling and programming that it enables to oversee more clearly. Note that, this task should not be confused with the alignment between ontologies or owl/rdf files [21][22] since here it is rather an alignment between the CIDOC-CRM ontology and raw data from databases or XML files (in our context, XML-EAD files).

Primarily, the mapping consists in filling a semantic graph's nodes. Terminal nodes will be filled with values extracted from data logical structures of the corresponding sub-projects whereas non-terminal or intermediary nodes will be filled with URIs and will then define by that means paths to terminal nodes. Note that a particular attention must be drawn to the construction of URIs for their readability, as well as for the consistency of graph's paths in order to avoid paths' conflicts and warrant the uniqueness of a given path compared to another.

Figure 7 illustrates an extract of data mapping, initially in XML-EAD [17] and that corresponds to the first theme of our semantic modelling (see Figure 3). In XML-EAD, for instance, dimensions of an object is obtained with xpath */ead/archdesc/did/physdesc/dimensions* or */ead/archdesc/dsc/c/did/physdesc/dimensions*, according to the target information level that can be either the collection level or the document level.

Hence, to describe the dimensions of an object, we use a sequence of triples of the form:

[http://www.modref.org/biblionum/document_id/e70_thing, rdf : type, ecrm : E70_Thing],

[http://www.modref.org/biblionum/document_id/e70_thing, ecrm : P43_has_dimension, http://www.modref.org/biblionum/document_id/e54_dimension],

[http://www.modref.org/biblionum/document_id/-e54_dimension, rdf : type, ecrm : E54_Dimension],

[http://www.modref.org/biblionum/document_id/-e54_dimension, rdfs : label, "/ead/archdesc/dsc/c/did/physdesc/dimensions"],

[http://www.modref.org/biblionum/document_id/e71_man-made_thing, owl : sameAs, http://www.modref.org/biblionum/document_id/e70_thing].

Finally, the mapping realised will be translated into a programmatic data structure that will be then used to automatically generate files that follow RDF and CIDOC-CRM syntax: it is the data migration into triplestores or the creation of triplestores.

V. Data Migration into triplestores

Efficiently migrating data into triplestores involves various skills. The sustainability of the whole procedure implies to define a general and rigorous architecture for the workflow of the different types of data handled. This architecture explicits the global method applied to all projects that wish to move their data into triplestores. This method is subdivided in different well-identified steps: data preparating (study and structural description), semantic modelling and data mapping from structural to semantic description and at last creating and exhibiting triplestores that can then be visualised and queried by users or semantic web applications. Initially, data are often non-structured or semi-structured (notes, reports, books, html) and first need to be converted into a structured representation (spreadsheets, databases, XML files) in order to easily construct their semantic representation thereafter. This continuum of steps requires several skills and needs some of in-between profiles skills to enable moving data from one format to another: (1) non-structured data or semi-structured data to structured data; (2) structured data to semantic data.

Besides, the key element of the architecture for migrating data into triplestores is the modelling and mapping of data with the semantic graph model chosen. In order to achieve data migration of ModRef project, we have performed an alignment between their data structural description and their semantic description by filling some nodes of the semantic graph with data retrieved from databases or collections of XML-EAD files. This migration into triplestores implies at the same time the reading of databases and the parsing of XML-EAD files (see Table I). Nodes filled with values are terminal nodes and non-terminal nodes are filled with URIs.

The proof of concept of ModRef or the validation of data migration into triplestores is a set of tasks uphill (preparating and structuring of data, semantic modelling, alignment of data) and downhill (publishing, visualising, querying and exploring triplestores) the migration process. Hence, exploiting triplestores by querying and exploring them and the avantages that can be got through triplestores is the other major aspect around those new data warehouses of RDF documents.

VI. Visualisation and Exploitation of triplestores

Created triplestores are available for visualising (under three different ways: rdf, triples and attribute-value summary) and querying through our web application. The interest of triplestores is that we have a public and published model of information representation that enables querying triplestores indifferently with the same procedures. We have defined two procedures for exploiting triplestores: interfaces similar to "general query forms" and "Endpoint Sparql" (see Figure 8).

As they are really close to natural language, "general query forms" are simple and intuitive means for querying triplestores. Special knowledge is not necessary, all that is needed is to fill target fields on a given form and launch the query execution. A Sparql query is automatically constructed using values of filled fields and the query obtained is then used to retrieve information from triplestores. At the end of query execution, a list of objects is selected and returned as results to the user who can then visualise them in three ways: *rdf, triples and attribute-value summary*.

Besides, we can also query triplestores by using "Endpoint Sparql". This second query mode requires Sparql query language knowledge that is, at present, the reference language for querying RDF documents. Sparql is a simple language but not always at everyone's comprehension level. Hence, "general query forms" can be seen as a first query step for triplestores whereas "Endpoint Sparql" guarantee a more complete exploitation of triplestores by a free formulation of Sparql "Select" query type.

Our web application allows to visualise, query and explore triplestores separately for each pilot project of ModRef but also together by using the LOD (Linked Open Data) of ModRef. The web application provides, for each project and for the LOD of ModRef, a service to visualise triplestores data under three forms but also provides a service to query triplestores by using either "general query forms" or "Endpoint Sparql". Hence, as results to a query, the LOD allows to retrieve various information (statue, tablet) coming from different triplestores (see Figure 8). Several Sparql queries have been executed to validate data migration and a list of queries samples is provided with the web application. We have developped our own web application "Endpoint Sparql" and we also provide a Virtuoso "Endpoint Sparql" (Virtuoso is a software that allows to create an instance of "Endpoint Sparql") [23].

Note that, the notion of exploiting triplestores refers to notions of querying and exploring semantic graphs. Hence, querying triplestores is executing Sparql queries that are pre-defined (general query forms) or free (Endpoint Sparql) whereas exploring triplestores is a kind of querying only performed through "Endpoint Sparql" for it allows to discover various paths in a semantic graph towards a given data. Actually, different paths can lead to the same information inside a graph (by the use of various notions: shortcut, refinement, entailment, inverse) even if those paths are not always all filled. We can then write Sparql queries to discover if different paths that lead to a given data exist or write queries to know paths

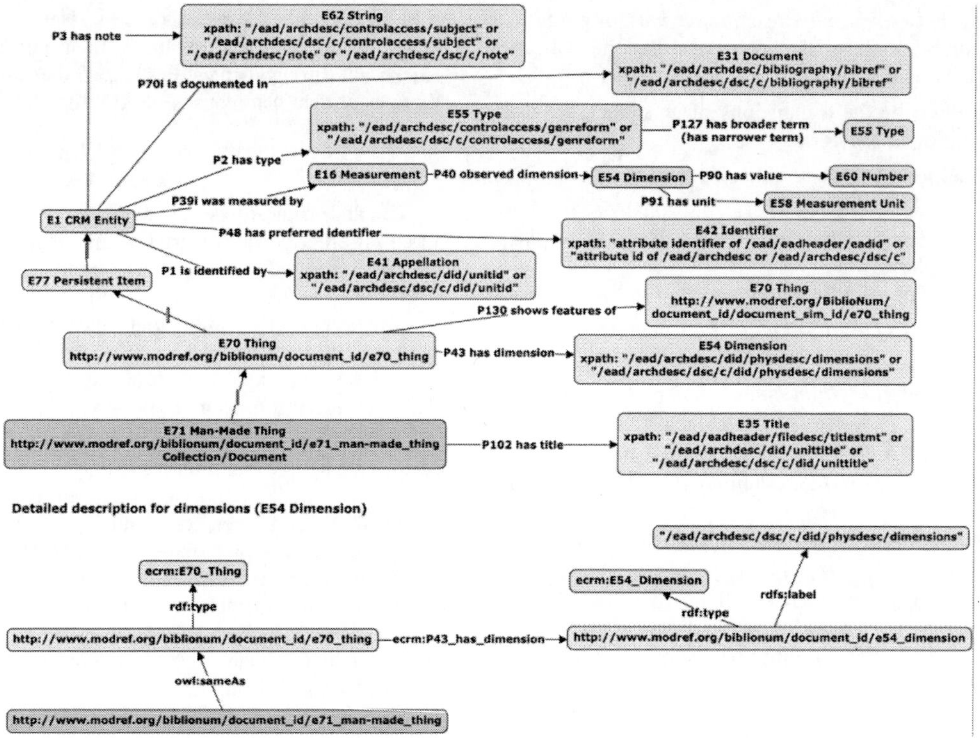

Figure 7. Data mapping snippet between XML-EAD and CIDOC-CRM.

that lead to terminal nodes associated to values. Exploring is then very important to master a specific triplestore.

VII. EVALUATION PROCEDURE AND RESULTS

We have perform several Sparql queries types to validate the various datasets of our triplestores. The queries can be divided into two groups, one group related to the general RDF syntax schema (*list of concepts or predicates used, list of terminal triples (see Table II), list of triples of a given resource, extracts of paths leading to non-empty terminal nodes*) and another group related to the CIDOC-CRM schema (*checking instanciation of a given class, checking labels of given entity or resource (see Table III), characteristics of a given object (see Table IV), information on origin or custody of a given object*).

TABLE II. LIST OF TERMINAL TRIPLES WHERE THE TERMINAL NODE IS NON-EMPTY.

```
SELECT Distinct ?subject ?predicate ?object
WHERE
{
?subject ?predicate ?object .
Filter ( isLiteral(?object) && ?object != "" )
}
```

Moreover, triplestores are subdivided into constant parts (number of objects or triples) and queries are executed each time on one part and gradually on the other parts if the user asks so. The results are then progressively merge. The user chooses to execute its queries bit by bit and can stop

TABLE III. LIST OF TYPES OR CATEGORIES OF OBJECTS.

```
PREFIX ecrm: <http://erlangen-crm.org/150929/>
PREFIX rdf: <http://www.w3.org/1999/02/22-rdf-syntax-ns#>
PREFIX rdfs: <http://www.w3.org/2000/01/rdf-schema#>

SELECT Distinct ?type
WHERE
{
?type_uri rdf:type ecrm:E55_Type .
?type_uri rdfs:label ?type .
Filter ( ?type != "" )
}
```

the execution on any part of the triplestore. The current part number (on which the current query has been executed) and the total number of parts are always shown. Figure 9 shows that queries average time execution (in seconds) is rather constant on a given triplestore's part (*1000 objects, approximately 100 000 triples*) and the execution speed of these queries is quite good for the users. Therefore, the cumulative time execution increases as triplestore's parts are combined.

Once the modelling and alignment tasks were done, we proceeded to the implementation of the architecture of the migration process and thereafter we implemented the modules for visualising and querying (General Query Form, Endpoint Sparql) triplestores. All these implementations took about one year. The time execution of the migration process itself, on a 2.13 GHz processor with 4 GB RAM, takes: 6 hours for the project *CDLI* involving one long SQL query; 30 minutes for the project *ObjMythArcheo* involving 32 SQL queries; 2 hours

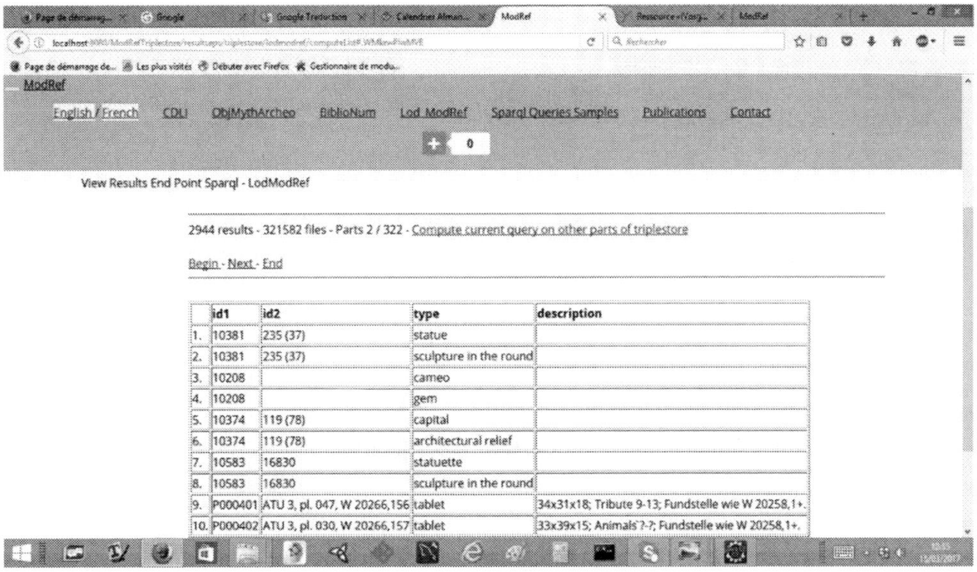

Figure 8. ModRef Project Web Application: Endpoint Sparql.

TABLE IV. LIST OF CHARACTERISTICS THAT COME FROM ROOT ENTITY "E1 CRM Entity".

```
PREFIX ecrm: <http://erlangen-crm.org/150929/>
PREFIX rdf: <http://www.w3.org/1999/02/22-rdf-syntax-ns#>
PREFIX rdfs: <http://www.w3.org/2000/01/rdf-schema#>

SELECT Distinct ?id1 ?id2 ?type ?description
WHERE
{
?e1_obj ecrm:P48_has_preferred_identifier ?id1_uri .
?id1_uri rdfs:label ?id1 .
?e1_obj ecrm:P1_is_identified_by ?id2_uri .
?id2_uri rdfs:label ?id2 .
?e1_obj ecrm:P2_has_type ?type_uri .
?type_uri rdfs:label ?type .
?e1_obj ecrm:P3_has_note ?description .
}
```

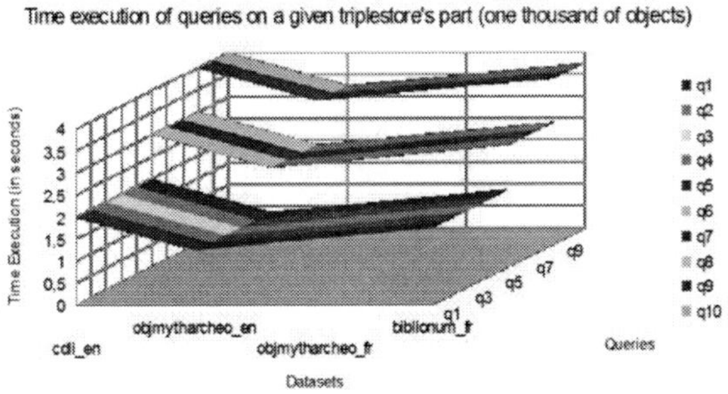

Figure 9. Queries Execution for ModRef Project.

for the project *BiblioNum* involving 36 XML-EAD paths.

Table V describes general statistics of the migration results for the three pilot projects of ModRef based on the following criteria: number of logical structure queries, number of

TABLE V. MIGRATION PROCEDURE GENERAL STATISTICS.

	CDLI	ObjMythArcheo	BiblioNum
Number of Logical Structure Queries	1 SQL query	32 SQL queries	36 XML-EAD paths
Number of Resources	36 000 000	840 000	6 300 000
Number of Literal Values	5 300 000	280 000	930 000
Number of Concepts	36	36	36
Number of Predicates	39	39	39

resources, number of literal values, number of concepts and predicates.

VIII. Conclusion

The ModRef project allows to realise the proof of concept (POC) of data migration into CIDOC-CRM triplestores through: a general architecture that identifies the various steps; modelling and data mapping with the CIDOC-CRM semantic graph; data migration into triplestores; publishing of triplestores through a bilingual "*English-French*" web application [7] that provides services for visualising, querying and exploring triplestores.

Further work is directed towards:

1) *improving the sharing, exchange and discovery of knowledge at a greater scale* by integrating other internet LOD (Linked Open data) [24][25]. LOD should increase the discovery of new knowledge, because of the amount and diversity of linked data but mainly due to the use of semantic web formalisms, metadata languages, thesaurus published, standardised and even normalised;
2) *comparison of various triplestores* that describe similar data [26] (similar objects, objects of same historical period, objects of same type, identical objects) in a LOD context. This will lead to mutual enrichment of the various actors of the LOD.

ACKNOWLEDGMENT

The author would like to thank the laboratory Labex "Les passés dans le présent" of the University of Paris 10 and the ANR project ModRef referenced by ANR-11-LABX-0026-01.

REFERENCES

[1] D. Oldman, M. Doerr, G. de Jong, B. Norton, and T. Wikman, "Realizing lessons of the last 20 years : A manifesto for data provisioning and aggregation services for the digital humanities. http://www.dlib.org/dlib/july14/oldman/07oldman.html [retrieved: March, 2017]," D-Lib Magazine, vol. 20, no. 7/8, 2014.

[2] P. L. Boeuf, M. Doerr, C. E. Ore, and S. Stead, "Definition of the cidoc conceptual reference model, version 6.2," Produced by the ICOM/CIDOC Documentation Standards Group, Continued by the CIDOC CRM Special Interest Group. http://www.cidoc-crm.org/ [retrieved: March, 2017], May 2015.

[3] S. V. Hooland and R. Verborgh, Linked Data for Libraries, Archives and Museums. How to Clean, Link and Publish Your Matadata, A. L. Association, Ed., 2014.

[4] N. Shadbolt, T. Berners-Lee, and W. Hall, "The semantic web revisited," IEEE Intelligent Systems, vol. 21, no. 3, 2006, pp. 96–101.

[5] T. Berners-Lee, J. Hendler, and O. Lassila, "The semantic web," Scientific American, 2001, pp. 34–43.

[6] T. Berners-Lee, "Axioms, architecture and aspirations," W3C all-working group plenary Meeting. https://www.w3.org/2001/Talks/0228-tbl/slide1-0.html [retrieved: March, 2017], 2001.

[7] "Modref cidoc-crm project," http://triplestore.modyco.fr [retrieved: March, 2017].

[8] R. Heartfield and G. Loukas, "A taxonomy of attacks and a survey of defence mechanisms for semantic social engineering attacks," ACM Computing Surveys (CSUR) - DL (Digital Library), vol. 48, no. 3, 2016.

[9] J. Scarinci and T. Myers, "A semantic web framework to enable sustainable lodging best management practices in the usa," Information Technology and Tourism, vol. 14, no. 4, 2014, pp. 291–315.

[10] "Cidoc-crm implementation," http://www.erlangen-crm.org/ [retrieved: March, 2017], 2015.

[11] "British museum cidoc-crm project," http://collection.britishmuseum.org/ [retrieved: March, 2017].

[12] "Arches cidoc-crm project," http://www.getty.edu/conservation/our_projects/field_projects/arches/ [retrieved: March, 2017].

[13] "Dbpedia project," http://www.dbpedia.org/sparql [retrieved: March, 2017].

[14] T. Ruan, Y. Li, H. Wang, and L. Zhao, "From queriability to informativity, assessing "quality in use" of dbpedia and yago," In proceedings of the 13th Extended Semantic Web Conference ESWC'16, 2016, pp. 52–68.

[15] "Nakala project," http://www.nakala.fr/sparql [retrieved: March, 2017].

[16] P. Haase, J. Broekstra, A. Eberhart, and R. Volz, "Comparison of rdf query languages," In proceedings of the third International Semantic Web Conference ISWC'04, 2004, pp. 502–517.

[17] "Xml-ead elements," https://www.loc.gov/ead/tglib/element_index.html [retrieved: March, 2017].

[18] "Cdli cidoc-crm project," http://www.cdli.ucla.edu [retrieved: March, 2017].

[19] "Objmytharcheo cidoc-crm project," http://www.limc-france.fr and http://medaillesetantiques.bnf.fr [retrieved: March, 2017].

[20] "Biblionum cidoc-crm project," http://www.argonnaute-u.paris10.fr [retrieved: March, 2017].

[21] D. Faria, C. Martins, and A. Nanavaty, "Agreementmakerlight results for oaei 2014," ISWC Workshop on Ontology Matching - Proceedings of the 9th International Conference on Ontology Matching (OM'14), vol. 1317, 2014, pp. 105–112.

[22] D. Faria, C. Pesquita, E. Santos, M. Palmonari, I. Cruz, and F. Couto, "The agreementmakerlight ontology matching system," The 12th International Conference on Ontologies, DataBases, and Applications of Semantics (ODBASE), 2013, pp. 527–541.

[23] "Modref virtuoso endpoint sparql," http://3s-passespresent.huma-num.fr/sparql [retrieved: March, 2017].

[24] W. Beek, L. Rietveld, S. Schlobach, and F. van Harmelen, "Lod laundromat: Why the semantic web needs centralization (even if we don't like it)," IEEE Internet Computing, vol. 20, no. 2, 2016, pp. 78–81.

[25] E. Daga, M. d'Aquin, A. Adamou, and S. Brown, "The open university linked data - data.open.ac.uk. semantic web," Semantic Web, vol. 7, no. 2, 2016, pp. 183–191.

[26] W. Beek, S. Schlobach, and F. van Harmelen, "A contextualised semantics of owl:sameas," In proceedings of the 13th Extended Semantic Web Conference ESWC'16, 2016, pp. 405–419.

AUTHOR INDEX

International Academy, Research,
and Industry Association (IARIA)
412 Derby Way
Wilmington, DE 19810

ISBN 978-1-5108-4300-4

CURRAN ASSOCIATES INC.
proceedings.com

14th International Joint Conference on Natural Language Processing and the 4th Conference of the Asia-Pacific Chapter of the Association for Computational Linguistics (IJCNLP-AACL 2025)

Student Research Workshop

Mumbai, India
20-24 December 2025